The Focus *of Our* Faith

Paul's Letter to the
Jesus Believers
at Colosse

*Bite~Sized Studies Through
the Book of Colossians*

Jeff Doles

The Focus of Our Faith

© 2012 by Jeff Doles

Published by
Walking Barefoot Ministries
P.O. Box 1062, Seffner, FL 33583

ISBN: 978-0-9823536-3-9

Scripture quotations marked *JVD* are rendered by the author.

For more resources on enjoying new life in Christ, living in faith and the power of the Holy Spirit, or to find out more about Jeff Doles, visit our websites:

www.WalkingBarefoot.com
www.TheFaithLog.com
www.JeffDoles.com

Contents

Introduction ~ Jesus Above All   7

Colossians 1:1   *Taken By Surprise*   11

Colossians 1:1-2   *Building Relationship at Colosse*   13

Colossians 1:2   *Father's Blessing*   16

Colossians 1:3-5   *The Divine Power Trio*   17

Colossians 1:5   *Heaven as Your Source*   19

Colossians 1:5-6   *Be Fruitful and Fill the Earth*   21

Colossians 1:7-8   *Fellow Servant, Faithful Discipler*   24

Colossians 1:8   *Love for the Saints, Love in the Spirit*   26

Colossians 1:9   *Filled with the Knowledge of God's Will*   28

Colossians 1:10   *A Walk Worthy*   31

Colossians 1:10   *A Life Pleasing*   33

Colossians 1:10   *A Life of Fruitfulness*   35

Colossians 1:10   *Every Good Work*   38

Colossians 1:10   *Knowing God More and More*   40

Colossians 1:11   *Empowered with All Power*   42

Colossians 1:11   *Putting Up with Joy*   45

Colossians 1:12   *Fully Qualified for the Father's Inheritance*   48

Colossians 1:13-14   *Into the Kingdom of Light*   50

Colossians 1:15-16   *The Image of the Invisible*   53

Colossians 1:17   *How All Things Hold Together*   55

Colossians 1:18   *The Incomparability of Divine Life*   58

Colossians 1:19   *Where All Divine Fullness Dwells*   60

Colossians 1:19-20   *Reconciling Heaven and Earth*   62

Colossians 1:19-20   *The Gospel of God's Pleasure*   65

Colossians 1:21-23   *Once Alienated, Now Unaccusable*   67

Colossians 1:23   *Continue in the Faith*   70

Colossians 1:24   *Filling Up the Afflictions of Messiah*   72

Colossians 1:25-26   *Stewards of Divine Mysteries*   75

Colossians 1:27   *The Revelation of Divine Glory in You*   78

Colossians 1:28   *Presenting Everyone Perfect*   81

Colossians 1:29   *His Energy Energizing Me*   83

Colossians 2:1-3   *Hidden Treasures of Wisdom and Knowledge*   85

Colossians 2:2   *Woven Together in Love*   88

Colossians 2:4-5   *Holding Steady Together*   90

Colossians 2:6   *Walking It Out*   91

Colossians 2:6-7   *Rooted and Built Up in Jesus*   93

Colossians 2:8   *Don't Be Plundered*   96

Colossians 2:9-10   *His Fullness and Ours*   98

Colossians 2:11   *Circumcision of the Heart*   100

Colossians 2:12   *Buried with Him, Raised with Him*   103

Colossians 2:13   *Side Slips Forgiven*   106

Colossians 2:14   *The Great Wipe Out*   107

Colossians 2:15   *Disarming the Powers*   109

Colossians 2:16-17   *Out of the Shadows*   112

Colossians 2:18-19   *Keeping Focus*   114

Colossians 2:20-23   *Live as Free*   115

Colossians 3:1-2   *Living from a Higher Realm*   117

Colossians 3:3-4   *Hidden in God*   120

Colossians 3:5-7   *Putting Old Ways to Death*   123

Colossians 3:8-11   *A Renewed Image*   126

Colossians 3:12-14   *Clothes for Your New Life*   129

Colossians 3:15-17   *The Word That Qualifies Us*   131

Colossians 3:18-4:1   *New Life in the Home*   133

Philemon   *Onesimus and Philemon ~ Receiving a Brother*   137

Colossians 4:2-4   *The Spiral of Watchful, Thankful Prayer*   140

Colossians 4:5-6   *Walking in Wisdom, Seasoned With Salt*   142

Colossians 4:7-11   *Not a One Man Show*   144

Colossians 4:12-14   *Standing Firm*   147

Colossians 4:15-18   *Fulfilling the Ministry of Jesus*   149

Introduction ~ Jesus Above All

Focus is important. The better your focus, the more clearly you can see. But it is important that your focus be on the right thing because your direction will follow your focus. Focus on the wrong thing and it will lead you in the wrong direction. Fix your attention on the rearview mirror while you are driving and you might well end up in a ditch. But when your focus is clear and on the right thing, then you will be heading in the right direction.

The gospel of our faith is the good news announcement that the kingdom of God has come and Jesus is the Christ, the Messiah—which is to say, God's anointed King. He is the focus of our faith, not only the One upon *whom* we fix our attention but also the One *through* whom we view the whole world, to see more clearly and understand God's purpose with greater wisdom.

That is what Paul's letter to the Jesus believers at Colosse is about. During his time of ministry in Ephesus (about AD 54-56), Paul sent Epaphras to Colosse, Laodicea and Hierapolis to proclaim the good news and establish the Church in that region. About five years passed and Paul received a good report about the Jesus believers there, who were mostly from among the Gentiles, but also some from the Jews. But there was also some disturbing news: False teachers were coming in to undermine the work of the gospel and pull believers away from their focus on the Lord Jesus.

Though we do not know exactly who and what these teachers and their doctrines were, they perhaps represented an early form of Gnosticism, a movement that influenced various churches during the early centuries. Gnosticism viewed the spiritual realm as pure but the physical world as inherently evil. Salvation was understood as an escape of the soul from the material realm through esoteric knowledge about the "emanations" or hierarchies of divine beings that proceeded from God. Gnosticism seems to have developed as a blend of ideas, possibly from such sources as Jewish mysticism, Zoroastrianism, Greco-Roman "mystery" religions and Neo-Platonic thought. Although it was not a distinctive movement until the second century AD, the ideas that gave shape to it were circulating a good while before that.

Paul does not define this false teaching for us and he does not particularly address it head on. However, we can make out some of the nature of this error by clues here and there in his letter to the believers at Colosse. It seems to have been a mixture of three things:

- *Jewish legalism*—with an emphasis on things like circumcision, dietary laws, sabbaths and new moon celebrations (Colossians 2:16).
- *Pagan elements*—"according to the traditions of men, according to the basic principles of the world, and not according to Christ" (Colossians 2:8). The "basic principles of the world," particularly, seems to be a reference to pagan ideas of elemental spirits and hierarchies.
- *Christian veneer*—These false teachers smuggled their legalist/pagan mixture into the church under the guise of Christian doctrine, but were actually exalting angelic hierarchies above Jesus.

Though this was not full-formed Gnosticism, it does appear to have had strong tendencies in that direction. For this reason, I refer to it in this book as "gnostic," with a small "g" and used as an adjective.

As we work through this letter, we will see a number of "in Him" and "with Him" statements. It will help us see Paul's point if we read them with emphasis on the word "Him" (that is, "in *Him*," "with *Him*") to stand in strong contrast with the "basic principles of the world" and the erroneous emphasis on angels. This will also help us better understand, by a sort of mirroring technique, the error Paul addresses as he stresses its opposite, the all-encompassing truth God has revealed to us in the gospel: In and through Jesus the Messiah, God has accomplished everything that needs to be done in the world—He is all we need!

Paul's letter is *to* the Jesus believers at Colosse but it is *for* Jesus believers in all times and places. So his teachings, instructions and prayers have application for us today. This book is a study of that letter and those teachings. It comes from a series I taught on Colossians in the Bible study group I have lead for over ten years. Teaching it live inspired me to expand on it in a series of blog posts at *www.TheFaithLog.com*. Now I have collected and edited them together into this present form (I believe in "retasking").

These are "bite-sized" studies to help guide you through Paul's letter a little at a time. For the most part, they retain the shape and style of the blog (minus the typos). At the end of each study, I have added some focus questions to help you think further about the truths Paul brings. There is no answer key (except Jesus). I have purposely left these questions open-ended to allow for maximum personal reflection and group discussion.

As you may notice, there is a bit of repetition in this book. Part of this is the nature of the blog posts, written with the expectation that this series would pick up new readers along the way, and a bit of repetition from previous posts would help them get "up to speed." On a few occasions, I have written about a particular passage more than once, approaching it from different angles. In Bible college, I had a professor who used to say, "Repetition is theological mucilage." There is a lot of truth in that, so I have let some of these repetitions stay to do their work and help sharpen our focus.

My intent with this book, as with my blog, is to encourage you and stir up your faith to receive the wonderful promises of God and walk in the divine destiny He has for you. For many years now, my favorite verse, the one I come back to again and again, is Isaiah 50:4. "The Lord GOD has given me the tongue of disciples, that I may know how to sustain the weary one with a word. He awakens me morning by morning, He awakens my ear to listen as a disciple" (*NASB*). That has been my desire with this project and, indeed, with all my writing and ministry—to sustain the weary one with a word.

Taken By Surprise

Paul, an apostle of Jesus the Messiah, by the will of God.
(Colossians 1:1 JVD)

Nobody was more surprised than Paul that he should be an apostle
of Jesus the Messiah, and that this was the will of God. He had
once been very violently opposed to Jesus and those who followed
Him as Messiah. This was back when Paul was known as Saul.

As for Saul, he made havoc of the church, entering every house,
and dragging off men and women, committing them to prison.
(Acts 8:3)

Then Saul, still breathing threats and murder against the disciples
of the Lord, went to the high priest and asked letters from him to
the synagogues of Damascus, so that if he found any who were of
the Way, whether men or women, he might bring them bound
to Jerusalem. (Acts 9:1-2)

But then, of course, Saul had his "Damascus road experience"—which was the *original* Damascus road experience. He had a dramatic encounter with Jesus. The story is told in Acts 9. As Saul came near the city, a bright light shone around him and he fell to the ground. He heard a voice speaking to him.

"Saul, Saul, why are you persecuting Me?"

"Who are You, Lord?" Saul asked.

"I am Jesus, whom you are persecuting."

"Lord, what do You want me to do?"

"Arise and go into the city, and you will be told what you must do."

Saul, his eyes blinded by that moment, continued on to Damascus, not knowing what would happen next. There was a man there named Ananias, whom the Lord Jesus directed to go to Saul, lay hands on him and restore his sight. Ananias did not understand why, because he had heard of how Saul had persecuted Jesus' followers at Jerusalem. The Lord answered, "Go, for he is a chosen vessel of Mine to bear My name before Gentiles, kings, and the children of Israel. For I will show him how many things he must suffer for My name's sake."

Ananias went and Saul was healed. Immediately Saul went to the synagogues of Damascus and began to preach that Jesus is the Son of God. He became part of the very movement he had originally intended to rub out there. Now he himself became a target and the Jewish leaders plotted to kill him. But the believers helped him get away safely.

Saul went back to Jerusalem to join with the believers there, the ones he had once persecuted. But his former reputation was still with him and the disciples at Jerusalem feared him. They did not believe he was now one of them. But Barnabas took him before the apostles and told them what had happened, how Saul had seen the Lord on the road to Damascus, how he had preached the name of Jesus boldly there and was himself persecuted for it. Then the believers at Jerusalem received him as a disciple.

So now in his letter to the believers at Colosse, Paul identifies himself, as he does in many of his other letters, as an apostle of Jesus the Messiah. He who had once rejected Jesus and persecuted His followers was now sent by Jesus to represent him before the nations.

It was the will of God that this should be, and no one was more surprised by it than Paul.

Focus Questions

1. What does it mean to be an apostle of Jesus the Messiah?

2. Why is it important that Paul was an apostle "by the will of God"?

3. How could God use someone who had been so vehemently against the people of King Jesus?

Building Relationship at Colosse

Paul, an apostle of Jesus Christ by the will of God, and Timothy our brother, to the saints and faithful brethren in Christ who are in Colosse. (Colossians 1:1-2)

Paul had never been to Colosse, but he spent an extended time in Ephesus, about 120 miles away, preaching and teaching about Jesus the Messiah. Luke records, "And this continued for two years, so that all who dwelt in Asia heard the word of the Lord Jesus, both Jews and Greeks" (Acts 19:10). The influence of Paul's ministry reached Colosse.

It was probably at this time that a man named Epaphras, of the region of Colosse, Laodicea and Hierapolis, heard Paul and became a believer in Jesus. Epaphras came home with the message of the gospel. Many there became believers and a church was started, meeting in a number of homes. Epaphras returned to Paul with news of their "love in the Spirit" (Colossians 1:8).

Now Paul sends them this letter. Notice, though, that it comes not just from Paul, but also from Timothy. This does not mean that Timothy actually composed any part of this letter, however, although he might well have served as Paul's secretary in putting pen to papyrus. So why does Paul mention him? He is building on relationship. Notice that he refers to Timothy as "*our* brother."

Timothy was himself converted by the ministry of Paul. Elsewhere, Paul calls him, "a true son in the faith" (1 Timothy 1:2). Timothy was native to the region and often travelled and served with Paul in his journeys throughout that land. So he would have been known *to* the Colossians and would probably also have been known *by* some, perhaps many, of them as well. By referring to him as "*our* brother," Paul immediately establishes a family bond between himself and the believers at Colosse.

In two brief sentences, the *From* and *To* slots of his letter, Paul connects with the Colossians in the *vertical* and *horizontal* dimensions. Vertically, Paul identifies himself as "an apostle of Jesus Christ by the will of God." He belongs to God. Apostleship was not something he took upon himself or, indeed, *could* have taken upon himself. It was something God did. "By the will of God," Paul says.

In a similar way, Paul addresses the Colossians as "saints"—holy ones! We often think of "saints" as some elite group of super spiritual Christians. But that is not what Paul has in mind. For him, everyday believers in Jesus the Messiah, from the greatest to the least (and without any consideration of greatness or leastness) are saints. To be holy simply means to be set apart for God. It is not something we do ourselves but something God Himself does for us. It is not based on our merit. God sets us apart for Himself because of His grace, which we receive by faith in Jesus the Messiah.

To be a saint, then, means to belong to God. Paul belonged to God and so did the believers at Colosse. And that is a very strong point of fellowship. This relationship has everything to do with Jesus the Messiah. It is *through* Him that Paul is an apostle, and it is *in* Him that the believers at Colosse have put their faith, and in whom they have been set apart for God.

Horizontally, Paul relates to the Colossian believers as brothers and sisters. He does this in two ways. The first is indirect: He calls Timothy "*our* brother." If you and I have the same brother, then we must be sisters and brothers also. The second way he demonstrates this relationship is explicit: He calls the saints at Colossae "faithful *brethren*" (brothers and sisters). They all share in the same devotion of faith with him.

The powerful truth of relationship in these opening verses is that all who put their faith in Jesus the Messiah belong to God and to each other as brothers and sisters.

Focus Questions

1. Why is Paul so keen on establishing relationship with the believers at Colosse?

2. Why is it important that this is a *familial* relationship, that is, of *brothers* and *sisters*?

3. How is Paul's apostleship like the holiness of these believers?

Father's Blessing

Grace to you and peace from God our Father and the Lord Jesus Christ. (Colossians 1:2)

After introducing himself to the Colossians as an apostle of Jesus the Messiah, and introducing himself and Timothy as faithful brothers in the Messiah, Paul offers a benediction, as he does so often in his letters. A benediction is a prayer of blessing. A common Jewish salutation in those days was "Greetings and peace." The Greek word for "greetings" is *chairein*, but Paul has replaced that with a related word, one that is theologically much more potent: *charis*—grace! Grace is the favor of God, who opens up all the resources of heaven on our behalf.

The Greek word for "peace" is *irene*, but Paul, being Jewish, no doubt has the Hebrew word *shalom* in mind, which is, again, more theologically profound. *Shalom* speaks of wholeness and restoration, the fullness of well-being, with nothing missing or broken. The *shalom* of God is the wholeness that comes from being in right relationship—in covenant relationship—with God.

The divine favor and wholeness of which Paul speaks comes from "God *our* Father." Here again, Paul signifies the relationship he has with the believers at Colosse: God is our Father. This speaks of family, of household, of inheritance. As believers in Jesus the Messiah, we each have a place in the family and a share in the abundance of the house. Paul teaches elsewhere that we share equally in the inheritance with Jesus Himself. "The Spirit Himself bears witness with our spirit that we are children of God, and if children, then heirs—heirs of God and joint heirs with Christ" (Romans 8:16-17).

Father's blessing of favor and wholeness comes to us also from the Son, Jesus the Messiah. The confession we make as Christians is that Jesus is Lord (Romans 10:9), which is to say that He is both God and King over all. It is through Him, through faith in Him, that we have wholeness in our relationship with God the Father and enjoy His favor.

Therefore, having been justified by faith, we have peace with God through our Lord Jesus Christ. (Romans 5:1).

Focus Questions

1. What difference does it make if someone speaks words of "grace" and "peace" to you?

2. Why is it important that this grace and peace comes from God as our *Father?*

3. Why is it important that it comes also from Jesus the Messiah?

The Divine Power Trio

We give thanks to the God and Father of our Lord Jesus Christ, praying always for you, since we heard of your faith in Christ Jesus and of your love for all the saints; because of the hope which is laid up for you in heaven, of which you heard before in the word of the truth of the gospel. (Colossians 1:3-5)

In rock and roll, a power trio is bass, guitar and drums (no rhythm guitar, no keyboard). But here Paul describes a different kind of power trio, one that comes from God. Having pointed out, in verses

1 and 2, his and their identity in God and extended to them the blessing of the Father, Paul now offers a word of thanksgiving to God for
the believers at Colosse. Three things stand out in them for which he
is especially grateful:

- ≈ Their faith in Jesus the Messiah.
- ≈ Their love for all the saints.
- ≈ The hope laid up for them in heaven.

Faith, hope, love. These are *huge* on Paul's list—and God's. They
are the "abiding" things. Remember how Paul ends his discourse on
love in 1 Corinthians 13. "Now abide faith, hope, love, these three;
but the greatest of these is love" (v. 13).

Notice, however, that Paul does not thank the Colossians themselves for these things, as if they somehow worked these things up
within themselves. No, he gives thanks to God, because they come
from Him. Faith comes by hearing and hearing by the Word of God
(Romans 10:17), which is given by inspiration of the Spirit of God.
Love is a fruit of the Holy Spirit (Galatians 5:22). Hope, which is a
positive expectation, a joyful anticipation, comes by the work of the
Spirit: "Now may the God of hope fill you with all joy and peace in
believing, that you may abound in hope by the power of the Holy
Spirit" (Romans 15:13). Because this is the work of God, and not of
ourselves, it is possible for faith, hope and love to be revealed in our
own lives. Our part is simply to yield to the work of God in us.

Faith, hope and love are a divine power trio. All three come from
God, and all three work together to release heaven on earth. Faith is
the underlying reality of things that are not yet apparent but which
we fully expect to see (Hebrews 11:1). However, faith without love is
meaningless and vain, of no value or profit (1 Corinthians 13:1-3). This

is because faith works through love, expressed and energized by love (Galatians 5:6). That is why, of the three, the greatest of these is love.

Focus Questions

1. How is faith revealed in the life of a Jesus believer?

2. How do we show our love for each other in practical ways?

3. How is faith expressed and energized by love?

Heaven as Your Source

Because of the hope which is laid up for you in heaven, of which you heard before in the word of the truth of the gospel. (Colossians 1:5)

In the Bible, hope is not wishful thinking or *maybe so/maybe not.* The biblical words for "hope" in the Old and New Testaments speak of expectation. Hope is a positive expectation, a joyful anticipation. Hope is about things that are not yet seen but which we fully expect to see. The author of Hebrews tells us that faith is the underlying reality of hope and the evidence of things not yet seen (Hebrews 11:1).

Paul gives thanks for the hope that belongs to the believers at Colosse, a hope "laid up for you in heaven." We often think of heaven merely in terms of destination, particularly as *future* destination. Many also often think of it as a place far, far away, somewhere out in space, at the edge of the universe or beyond.

For those who know Jesus the Messiah, though, heaven is a present reality. Paul tells us that God has blessed us with every spiritual blessing *in the heavenlies* (Ephesians 1:3), that He has made us alive together with Jesus the Messiah, raised us up together and made us sit together with Him *in the heavenlies* (Ephesians 2:5-6). Notice the tense. These are not future events but accomplished acts and present realities. They are both now and forever. Heaven is not far away—how can it be when we who are of earth have already been seated there with King Jesus? Think dimensionally instead or merely geographically.

Think also of heaven not merely as destination, but as source. Paul tells us that our citizenship is in heaven (Philippians 3:20). Although he traveled far and wide preaching the gospel, his citizenship was in Rome. That brought with it certain benefits and privileges, which Paul could invoke no matter where he was in the empire. Likewise, our citizenship in heaven brings with it certain benefits and privileges that we may call upon at any time, no matter where we are in the world. Heaven is not just our location—it is our source. Everything we need has already been provided for us by our Father in heaven.

We are people of heaven and earth. God's plan is that, in the end, heaven and earth will come together as one (see Revelation 21, which portrays the New Jerusalem, the city of heaven, coming down to unite with the earth). It has already begun. Jesus said, "From the days of John the Baptist until now, the kingdom of heaven has been forcefully advancing, and forceful men lay hold of it" (Matthew 11:12 *New International Version*). Our job is to lay hold of it by faith and to pray, as Jesus taught us, "Kingdom of God, come! Will of God, be done on earth as it is in heaven" (Matthew 6:10 *JVD*). The apostle John tells us, "The darkness is passing away, and the true light is already shining" (1 John 2:8).

These are all present realities, in process and coming to pass in the here and now. Though we do not see them all now, we can have every expectation that they will be revealed. As we joyfully anticipate the completion of what God has already begun, we can, by faith, draw on heaven as our source and supply. This is good news from the gospel.

Focus Questions

1. What is your expectation about what God has prepared for you?

2. How does hope change the way you live?

3. How does having heaven as your *source* change your expectation?

Be Fruitful and Fill the Earth

*Which you heard before in the word of the truth of the gospel, which has come to you, as it has also in all the world, and is bringing forth fruit, as it is also among you since the day you heard and knew the grace of God in truth. (Colossians 1:5-6)**

There is an interesting comparison between what Paul notes was already happening with the gospel and the divine mandate given to the first man and woman in Genesis 1. It is especially interesting when we remember that the gospel results in *new creation*: "Therefore, if anyone is in Christ, he is a new creation; old things have passed away; behold, all things have become new" (2 Corinthians 5:17). The

* Some early Greek manuscripts have an additional word. So the *NASB* translates, "constantly bearing fruit and increasing" (a margin note shows that this can also be rendered as "spreading abroad"). The *HCSB* has it as, "bearing fruit and growing all over the world."

one who trusts in Jesus the Messiah is not only a new creature himself but is part of the new creation that God has already begun through Jesus and which will culminate in a new heaven and a new earth. In 1 Corinthians 15:45, Paul compares Jesus to Adam: "So it is written, 'The first man Adam became a living being.' The last Adam became a life-giving spirit." Closer to home in the context of this letter, Paul calls Jesus "the firstborn over all creation" (Colossians 1:15).

When God created the first man and woman in the divine image and likeness, He blessed them and said to them, "Be fruitful and multiply; fill the earth and subdue it" (Genesis 1:28). Notice especially in this divine commission the idea of fruitfulness and of filling the earth. Do you hear the echoes of it in Colossians 1:6 with respect to the gospel, which even in Paul's own day was filling the world and bringing forth fruit?

In the beginning, God created the heavens and the earth, and He did it by the Word: "By faith we understand that the worlds were framed by the word of God" (Hebrews 11:3). The new creation comes the same way, by the Word of God, which Paul here calls the "word of the truth of the gospel." Jesus, who by His resurrection from the dead became the firstborn of the new creation, gathered His disciples and gave them this commission:

> *All authority has been given to Me in heaven and on earth. Go therefore and make disciples of all the nations, baptizing them in the name of the Father and of the Son and of the Holy Spirit, teaching them to observe all things that I have commanded you; and lo, I am with you always, even to the end of the age." (Matthew 28:18-20)*

This was already beginning to be fulfilled, as Paul attests. The gospel had come to Colosse, "as it has in all the world" and was bearing fruit, "as it is also among you since the day you heard and knew the grace of God in truth."

Let's take a moment and notice Paul's emphasis on "truth" here. The believers at Colosse heard the "word of the *truth* of the gospel" and they "heard and knew the grace of God in *truth*." Paul is beginning to introduce his reason for writing this letter. Later, he will address this purpose directly, and it has to do with the truth of the gospel over against the error of false teachers.

Paul says that they "heard" and "knew" the grace of God. The use of "heard" here does not mean that the gospel was merely spoken in the hearing of these Colossians but it indicates their receptivity to the good news. It means that they received it, embraced it, followed it, obeyed it. The Greek word for "knew" is not about a detached, theoretical knowledge but speaks of a personal, experiential knowledge. They embraced the truth of the gospel and experienced the grace of God for themselves.

Focus Questions

1. Nearly two thousand years later, how has the gospel come to you in your part of the world?

2. What is the fruit it has been bringing forth in you and in the world?

3. How have you experienced the grace of God in the truth of the gospel?

Fellow Servant, Faithful Discipler

As you also learned from Epaphras, our dear fellow servant, who is a faithful minister of Christ on your behalf, who also declared to us your love in the Spirit. (Colossians 1:7-8)

As the gospel, the *good news* about the grace of God through Jesus the Messiah, began to fill the world, it soon came to Colosse, where some believed. Ever since then, Paul says, it has been bringing forth fruit among them. The grace of God is not a one-off experience where you hear the good news, believe it and that's that. That is just the beginning. There is a new life and a new way of living. The grace of God continues to work, bearing its fruit in us. In Galatians, Paul speaks of the fruit of the Spirit: love, joy, peace, longsuffering, kindness, goodness, gentleness, faithfulness, self-control (Galatians 5:22-23). The grace of God is a tree of life within us and the process of learning to walk in this grace and experience this fruit is called *discipleship*.

"You *learned* this from Epaphras," Paul says. The Greek word for "learn" is *manthano*. From it comes the word *mathetes*, the Greek word for "disciple." The believers at Colosse were discipled, taught how to live in the grace of God, by Epaphras. So who is this guy?

- ❧ He is one of their own, a man of Colosse—"one of you," Paul says (Colossians 4:12)—who ministers throughout the region, in Laodicea and Hierapolis (4:13).
- ❧ He is a well-loved "fellow servant" with Paul and Timothy, and indeed with all who serve Jesus the Messiah.
- ❧ He is a faithful "minister."
- ❧ He is a man of fervent prayer and great zeal (4:12-13).
- ❧ Not only a fellow servant, he is also a "fellow prisoner" with Paul.

That's what Paul calls him in his brief letter to Philemon (v. 23), one of the believers living near Colosse. Paul wrote both of these letters, as well as the ones to believers at Ephesus and Philippi, while he was in prison for proclaiming King Jesus.

Notice that Paul calls Epaphras both a "fellow servant" (Greek, *syndoulos*, slaves together) and a faithful "minister" (Greek, *diakonos*, deacon). *Vine's Complete Expository Dictionary of Old and New Testament Words* explains the difference between these two words this way:

> *Diakonos* is, generally speaking, to be distinguished from *doulos*, "a bondservant, slave"; *diakonos* views a servant in relationship to his work; *doulos* views him in relationship to his master. See, e.g., Matt. 22:2-14; those who bring in the guests (vv. 3-4, 6, 8, 10) are *douloi*; those who carry out the king's sentence (v. 13) are *diakonoi*.

Servant speaks of the One to whom Epaphras belongs—King Jesus the Messiah. *Minister* speaks of the function he performs, the service he renders to Jesus and His church. It is a work in which he has been found to be faithful, trustworthy, loyal. He did not just introduce the Colossians to Jesus; he ministered the grace and hospitality of Jesus to them. With fervent prayer and great zeal, he discipled them in faith, hope and love and became the founding pastor of the Church at Colosse.

Focus Questions

1. Who are the people who have been faithful in ministering the things of Jesus to you, teaching you how to live in the grace of God?

2. Is being a servant of King Jesus only for the trained, anointed or appointed?

3. Who are the people for whom you have the opportunity to be a faithful minister of King Jesus?

Love for the Saints, Love in the Spirit

Who also declared to us your love in the Spirit. (Colossians 1:8)

In verse 4, Paul gave thanks to God for the believers in Colosse, for their faith, their hope and their "love for all the saints." Not just for their own little group, but for *all* the saints.

Love does not take offense, keep score or bear grudges—there is no place for unforgiveness in love. Instead,

> *Love suffers long and is kind; love does not envy; love does not parade itself, is not puffed up; does not behave rudely, does not seek its own, is not provoked, thinks no evil; does not rejoice in iniquity, but rejoices in the truth; bears all things, believes all things, hopes all things, endures all things. (1 Corinthians 13:4-7)*

On the night of the Last Supper, the night He washed the disciples feet, the night before He went to the cross, Jesus said to the disciples, "This is My commandment, that you love one another as I have loved you. Greater love has no one than this, than to lay down one's life for his friends" (John 15:12-13).). I call it the *algebra* of love: God is love; love gives and serves. That is, "God is love" (1 John 4:8) and it is the nature of love to give and serve. "God so loved the world that

He *gave* His only begotten Son" (John 3:16). "The Son of Man did not come to be served, but to *serve*, and to *give* His life a ransom for many" (Mark 10:45). Jesus calls us by this love, and He calls us to show this same love to each other.

How does it happen? Where do we find the kind of love with which to love everyone in this way? Paul leads us to the answer. In Colossians 1:7-8, he speaks of Epaphras, one of their own, who "declared to us your love in the Spirit." Paul presents us with two aspects of love. Where verse 4 speaks of the *object* of their love, "all the saints," verse 8 identifies the *source* of their love, "in the Spirit."

Love is the "fruit of the Spirit," Paul tells us (Galatians 5:22). Now, fruit is not something that you clip *onto* the branches of a tree, but it arises *from within* the tree. Fruit is the abundance of the life that comes forth from the tree. That is the way it is with love; it arises from the Spirit of God within us. "Whoever confesses that Jesus is the Son of God, God abides in him, and he in God" (1 John 4:15). We are the temple of God, who is love, and the Spirit of God dwells in us (1 Corinthians 3:16). As we yield ourselves to God and allow the Holy Spirit to fill us and work in us, He brings forth the fruit of the Spirit, which is the character of Jesus, into our lives. So now it is possible for us to love in such a way and with such a depth we never could before.

Focus Questions

1. How and through whom have you experienced the love of God?

2. How do we connect with the source of love and let it flow through us?

3. Who around you needs a practical expression of God's love today and in what way can you bring it?

Filled with the Knowledge of God's Will

For this reason we also, since the day we heard it, do not cease to pray for you, and to ask that you may be filled with the knowledge of His will in all wisdom and spiritual understanding; that you may walk worthy of the Lord, fully pleasing Him, being fruitful in every good work and increasing in the knowledge of God; strengthened with all might, according to His glorious power, for all patience and longsuffering with joy; giving thanks to the Father who has qualified us to be partakers of the inheritance of the saints in the light. (Colossians 1:9-12)

Paul is thankful to God for the community of believers at Colosse, for their faith in Jesus the Messiah, their love for all the saints, the hope laid up in heaven for them, and their love in the Spirit. Prayers of thanksgiving, such as offered in Colossians 1:3-4, are about where we have been and where we are now, and they are quite wonderful in themselves. However, Paul now takes a turn in his prayer for believers, a prayer to launch us into where we are going. It is a *pastoral* turn, so I call the prayer in this next section, Colossians 1:9-12, a *pastoral* prayer.

In Greek, the word for "pastor" is the word for "shepherd." That is what a pastor is, a shepherd. The concern of the pastor/shepherd is to guide the sheep to good pasture and protect them from wolves. It will become apparent, as we continue in this letter, that Paul sees wolves (false teachers) circling and that he is writing to protect the sheep and direct them to safe feeding ground.

In his pastoral prayer for believers, Paul asks the Father that we may be filled with the knowledge of His will "in all wisdom and understanding." First, note the word "filled" (Greek, *pleroo*, pronounced with three syllables). The idea of *fullness* shows up a number of times in this letter. This suggests that one of the errors Paul may be addressing is an early gnostic teaching that one can have the fullness of divine blessing through the legalistic and pagan notions being introduced to the Colossian believers by false teachers.

"Be filled" is passive, not active. We cannot fill ourselves with the knowledge of God's will, for who knows the mind of God except God? No, God is the one who must fill us; our part is simply to let Him, to look to Him and to yield to Him in everything. As we yield to the fullness that comes from God, we will find all we need for the life God calls us to live.

Gnosticism (from the Greek word *gnosis*, "knowledge") taught that the universe was created imperfectly by demiurges, intermediaries or emanations of God, and that an esoteric knowledge of this was necessary in order to escape the bondage of the material world. One of the gnostic terms for God was *Pleroma*, which is the Greek word for "fullness."

Paul's message to the Colossians is that the fullness of God is not found through some special knowledge of divine emanations or through the exaltation of angels, but in knowing the will of God. But what is the will of God? Paul will come to that at the end of chapter 1, about "the mystery which has been hidden from ages and from generations, but now has been revealed to His saints. To them God *willed* to make known what are the riches of the glory of this mystery among the Gentiles: which is Christ in you, the hope of glory" (Colossians 1:26-27).

This is not an esoteric knowledge but a mystery, which is a secret God has revealed to *all* the saints (remember that "saints" does not refer to *elite* believers but to *all* believers, who have been made holy, set apart for God). The will of God has everything to do with this truth: "Christ in you, the hope of glory." In other words, it is in Jesus the Messiah, not in angels or hierarchies, that we have every expectation of the fullness of God's glory being revealed in us.

Paul's prayer for believers is that we may be filled with the knowledge of God's will. The Greek word for "knowledge" here is *epignosis*. It is a fullness of knowledge. Not some vague mental notion of God's will, but a personal, intimate experience of His desire and purpose. It is a personal, intimate experience of Jesus living in us by the Holy Spirit.

Wisdom and understanding helps us bring together what God is showing us, to see what it means, how it applies, what to do about it. This comes to us by the Holy Spirit ministering to our own spirits. The role of the Spirit is always to point us to Jesus. Speaking about the Spirit, Jesus said, "All things that the Father has are Mine. Therefore I said that He will take of Mine and declare it to you" (John 16:15). Here is the fullness of God revealed to us in the Son by the Holy Spirit.

In the mystery of God, which is freely given to every believer, and in Jesus the Messiah, who is revealed in us by the Holy Spirit, we find "all the treasures of wisdom and knowledge" (Colossians 2:3). Here is all the fullness, all the wisdom, all the knowledge we need. Not in angels or hierarchies, but in Jesus the Messiah. When we understand who Jesus is in us, individually and as the Church, we will understand what the will of God is about.

Focus Questions

1. Why is it important for believers to be filled with the knowledge of God's will?

2. Why does wisdom and understanding require the work of the Holy Spirit?

3. How is the will of God revealed in Jesus the Messiah?

A Walk Worthy

For this reason we also, since the day we heard it, do not cease to pray for you, and to ask that you may be filled with the knowledge of His will in all wisdom and spiritual understanding; that you may walk worthy of the Lord, fully pleasing Him, being fruitful in every good work and increasing in the knowledge of God; strengthened with all might, according to His glorious power, for all patience and longsuffering with joy; giving thanks to the Father who has qualified us to be partakers of the inheritance of the saints in the light. (Colossians 1:9-12)

Paul's prayer for Jesus believers is that we may be filled with the knowledge of God's will, so that we may "walk worthy of the Lord." By "walk," Paul means how we live, how we *do* life. Walking is a process, one step after another, "picking 'em up and putting 'em down." There is a consistent pattern to a proper walk, otherwise we stagger, limp along or stumble altogether.

A walk worthy of the Lord is a life that is appropriate and fitting for our relationship with God and who we are in Jesus the Messiah. This is important to Paul, and he speaks of it in some of his other letters.

I, therefore, the prisoner of the Lord, beseech you to walk worthy of the calling with which you were called, with all lowliness and gentleness, with longsuffering, bearing with one another in love, endeavoring to keep the unity of the Spirit in the bond of peace. (Ephesians 4:1-3)

You are witnesses, and God also, how devoutly and justly and blamelessly we behaved ourselves among you who believe; as you know how we exhorted, and comforted, and charged every one of you, as a father does his own children, that you would walk worthy of God who calls you into His own kingdom and glory. (1 Thessalonians 2:10-12)

Only let your conduct be worthy of the gospel of Christ, so that whether I come and see you or am absent, I may hear of your affairs, that you stand fast in one spirit, with one mind striving together for the faith of the gospel, and not in any way terrified by your adversaries. (Philippians 1:27-28)

What does it look like to walk worthy? Humbleness, gentleness, being patient and loving with each other, directing our energies to the unity and peace we share in the Spirit of God. Having one mind, one heart, one joint-desire, working together as one for the sake of making King Jesus known, so that we may manifest the kingdom and glory of God.

In his letter to the Jesus believers at Colosse, Paul focuses on five characteristics of a worthy walk, and we will look at these in more detail in the next sections.

- Fully pleasing to the Lord.
- Always bearing fruit in every good work.
- Always being increased in the knowledge of God.
- Always being strengthened with all might (Colossians 1:11)
- Always giving thanks to the Father (Colossians 1:11).

Notice that there is a fullness and a constancy to these things. It is a strong and steady walk Paul is talking about, but it is important to understand that we do not do this in our own strength or even in our own understanding. But we'll get to that in a later section.

Focus Questions

1. Why is it important to understand that walking is a *process*?

2. Why is *consistency* in our walk important?

3. Why it is important to understand that we do not walk this walk in our own strength?

A Life Pleasing

For this reason we also, since the day we heard it, do not cease to pray for you, and to ask ... that you may walk worthy of the Lord, fully pleasing Him. (Colossians 1:9-10)

In speaking of a walk that is worthy of the Lord and fully pleasing to Him, Paul has in mind the Lord Jesus as our example. We read in Colossians 1:19, "For it pleased the Father that in Him [Jesus] all the fullness should dwell." The ministry of Jesus, everything He did, was all about pleasing the Father:

- "Most assuredly, I say to you, the Son can do nothing of Himself, but what He sees the Father do; for whatever He does, the Son also does in like manner" (John 5:19).
- "I can of Myself do nothing. As I hear, I judge; and My judgment is righteous, because I do not seek My own will but the will of the Father who sent Me" (John 5:30).
- "For I have come down from heaven, not to do My own will, but the will of Him who sent Me" (John 6:38).

  "When you lift up the Son of Man, then you will know that I am He, and that I do nothing of Myself; but as My Father taught Me, I speak these things. And He who sent Me is with Me. The Father has not left Me alone, for I always do those things that please Him" (John 8:29).

So, Jesus is our prime example. But perhaps Paul was thinking also of Enoch, about whom the book of Genesis says: "Enoch lived sixty-five years, and begot Methuselah. After he begot Methuselah, Enoch walked with God three hundred years, and had sons and daughters. So all the days of Enoch were three hundred and sixty-five years. And Enoch walked with God; and he was not, for God took him" (Genesis 5:21-24).

Enoch walked with God all the days of his life. He did not die, however, but was simply *taken* by God. This was very unusual and, unsurprisingly, a Jewish theology developed around it. The author of Hebrews sums it up this way: "By faith Enoch was taken away so that he did not see death, 'and was not found, because God had taken him'; for before he was taken he had this testimony, that he pleased God" (Hebrews 11:5).

Enoch walked with God and had this testimony: He pleased God. Certainly, this was a walk worthy of the Lord—and *with* the Lord—but how did Enoch please God? It was by faith, as the author of Hebrews explains:

> *But without faith it is impossible to please Him, for he who comes to God must believe that He is, and that He is a rewarder of those who diligently seek Him. (Hebrews 11:6)*

Enoch believed God and because of that, God was pleased with him. In the Bible, faith is about believing God and His promises. It is

entrusting ourselves to Him and following what He says. Abraham believed God and it was reckoned to him as righteousness, that is, rightness with God (Genesis 15:6). For more examples, see Hebrews 11, which is full of Old Testament saints who pleased God by their faith in Him.

It is by faith that the Lord Jesus pleased the Father, believing everything He heard the Father say and do, then speaking and acting in agreement with the Father's will. That is how Jesus operated in both His divinity and His humanity, and that is how we, too, can live a life that is fully pleasing to God. By believing whatever He says and does, then speaking and living in agreement with it.

Focus Questions

1. Why is God pleased by faith?

2. How does faith result in obedience?

3. What do you hear the Father saying and see the Father doing today?

A Life of Fruitfulness

That you may walk worthy of the Lord … being fruitful. (Colossians 1:10)

In verse 6, Paul gave thanks to God that the gospel was *bearing fruit* and *being increased* all over the world, and that it had come to the Colossians. It echoes the mandate God first gave Adam and Eve in the Garden of Eden: "Be fruitful and multiply, fill the earth and subdue it" (Genesis 1:28). Now in verse 10, Paul picks up on that theme again in his pastoral prayer. He asks God that Jesus believers may be fruitful in every good work and increase in the knowledge of God.

God has always been interested in fruitfulness. In the beginning, He created all the plants to yield seed and trees to bear fruit and re-produce "according to their kind." He created all the creatures of the land, sea and air to reproduce "according to their kind." Last of all, He created man, male and female, to be fruitful and multiply.

Fruitfulness is also an important part of the series of blessings in Deuteronomy 28: "Blessed shall be the fruit of your body, the produce of your ground and the increase of your herds, the increase of your cattle and the offspring of your flocks" (Deuteronomy 28:4). It is also part of the happiness and prosperity of those who meditate on the instruction of the Lord.

> *He shall be like a tree*
> *Planted by the rivers of water,*
> *That brings forth its fruit in its season,*
> *Whose leaf also shall not wither;*
> *And whatever he does shall prosper.*
>
> *(Psalm 1:3)*

Then there is the teaching Jesus gave to the disciples on the night of the Last Supper, about the vine and the branches:

> *I am the vine, you are the branches. He who abides in Me, and I in him, bears much fruit; for without Me you can do nothing.*
> *By this My Father is glorified, that you bear much fruit; so you will be My disciples.*

You did not choose Me, but I chose you and appointed you that you should go and bear fruit, and that your fruit should remain, that whatever you ask the Father in My name He may give you. (John 15:5, 8, 16).

In Galatians, Paul talks about the "fruit of the Spirit," in contrast to the "works of the flesh."

But the fruit of the Spirit is love, joy, peace, longsuffering, kindness, goodness, faithfulness, gentleness, self-control. Against such there is no law. (Galatians 5:22-23)

This fruit cannot be produced by keeping laws or observing rules; it is the work of the Holy Spirit to bring forth this fruit, which is the character of Jesus. Fruit is the overflow of the life of the vine, the life of Jesus at work in us. Our part is to yield to this life and the fruit will come.

Focus Questions

1. Why is God so interested in fruitfulness?

2. What is the relationship between *fruit* and the *life* of the fruit-bearer?

3. Does a tree strain to bring forth its fruit?

Every Good Work

Being fruitful in every good work. (Colossians 1:10)

Now let's talk about "every good work." In Ephesians, Paul tells us
that salvation, grace and faith are the gift of God.

*For by grace you have been saved through faith, and that not of
yourselves; it is the gift of God, not of works, lest anyone should
boast. For we are His workmanship, created in Christ Jesus for
good works, which God prepared beforehand that we should walk
in them. (Ephesians 2:8-10).*

"Good works" are not the cause or basis of salvation but the result or benefit of salvation. They come from God, because we are His
workmanship, His "doing." They come through Jesus the Messiah,
because of the new life we have in Him and the life He lives in us.

"Every good work" is one of Paul's favorite phrases; we find it a
number of times in his letters. The author of Hebrews also uses it,
and in a way that sounds very much like Paul.

*And God is able to make all grace abound toward you, that
you, always having all sufficiency in all things, may have an
abundance for every good work. (2 Corinthians 9:8)*

*Now may our Lord Jesus Christ Himself, and our God and Fa-
ther, who has loved us and given us everlasting consolation and
good hope by grace, comfort your hearts and establish you in every
good word and work. (2 Thessalonians 2:16-17)*

All Scripture is given by inspiration of God, and is profitable for doctrine, for reproof, for correction, for instruction in righteousness, that the man of God may be complete, thoroughly equipped for every good work. (2 Timothy 3:16-17)

Remind them to be subject to rulers and authorities, to obey, to be ready for every good work, to speak evil of no one, to be peaceable, gentle, showing all humility to all men. (Titus 3:1-2)

Now may the God of peace who brought up our Lord Jesus from the dead, that great Shepherd of the sheep, through the blood of the everlasting covenant, make you complete in every good work to do His will, working in you what is well pleasing in His sight, through Jesus Christ, to whom be glory forever and ever. Amen. (Hebrews 12:20-21)

The grace of God supplies us, equips us, prepares us, establishes us and makes us complete in every good work. God even supplies for us in our finances (which is the context of 2 Corinthians 9) so that we may always have all we need, plus abundance so we have something to give for "every good work." It is the work of God at work in us to bring forth the fruit that consists of good works. He supplies the seed and even multiplies it to "increase the fruit of your righteousness, while you are enriched in everything for all liberality, which causes thanksgiving through us to God" (2 Corinthians 9:10-11). From beginning to end, it is God at work in us, to bless us and make us a blessing to others and a praise to Him.

"Every good work" does not mean always doing everything all the time. After all, we do have to sleep! What it does mean, though, is that no matter what times and circumstances we may find ourselves in, there is always something we can offer, some good we can do, some fruit we can bring forth to bless others. As we pay attention to where God has placed us, what He has supplied and how the Holy Spirit is working in us, and we yield ourselves to Him, God will lead us.

Focus Questions

1. What is the relationship between God's work and our work?

2. How do good works reveal King Jesus in the world?

3. What good work is God calling *you* to today?

Knowing God More and More

That you may walk worthy of the Lord ... increasing in the knowledge of God. (Colossians 1:9-10)

In verse 9, Paul speaks of being filled with the knowledge of God's will. In verse 10, he shifts the focus to knowing God Himself, and increasing that knowledge. The Greek word for "knowledge" is both cases is *epignosis*, which is about a depth or fullness of knowledge. This is not merely head knowledge, an accumulation of facts or even of understanding how those facts work together. It is not *theoretical* knowledge, but *experiential* knowledge. Not the kind of knowledge that puffs up, but knowledge that is according to love, which builds up. "Knowledge puffs up, but love edifies" (1 Corinthians 8:1). It is not merely knowing *about* God but knowing *God*, who *is* love.

Paul speaks of "increasing" in this knowledge. Actually in the

Greek text, this word is in the passive voice. That is, it is not something we do for ourselves but something that is done for us. We do not increase ourselves in the knowledge of God, we are increased in the knowledge of God. Only God can do that for us and He does it by the work of the Holy Spirit.

> *For what man knows the things of a man except the spirit of the man which is in him? Even so no one knows the things of God except the Spirit of God. Now we have received, not the spirit of the world, but the Spirit who is from God, that we might know the things that have been freely given to us by God.*
>
> *These things we also speak, not in words which man's wisdom teaches but which the Holy Spirit teaches, comparing spiritual things with spiritual. But the natural man does not receive the things of the Spirit of God, for they are foolishness to him; nor can he know them, because they are spiritually discerned. But he who is spiritual judges all things, yet he himself is rightly judged by no one. For "who has known the mind of the Lord that he may instruct Him?" But we have the mind of Christ. (1 Corinthians 2:11-16)*

Notice also that this increase is in the present tense; it speaks of continuous action. God's plan is that we are *always being increased* by Him in the knowledge of Him, continually knowing Him more and more. It is a growth process. Peter says, "But grow in the grace and knowledge of our Lord and Savior Jesus Christ" (2 Peter 3:18).

This is personal, intimate, revelation knowledge of God—He reveals Himself to us in personal, intimate relationship! Through Jesus, through the Spirit, through the Word. He fills us with the knowledge of His will, revealing His desire, revealing His heart. Every response we make to that revelation in faith, and the obedience of faith, will be pleasing to Him and will bear the fruit of good works He desires. A walk worthy *of* the Lord is all about walking *with* the Lord. The more we walk with Him, the more we will know Him. He will not hold back but will reveal Himself freely to us as we walk along with Him.

Focus Questions

1. What is the difference between knowing *about* a person and actually knowing the person himself?

2. How is it possible to know God Himself, and not just *about* Him?

3. Why is knowing God Himself important to having a walk worthy of Him?

Empowered with All Power

Strengthened with all might, according to His glorious power. (Colossians 1:11)

Paul prays for believers that we may be filled with the knowledge of God's will, and that we may have a walk worthy of the Lord. But there is something very important we need to understand about this walk:

THIS WALK IS NOT SOMETHING WE CAN DO IN OUR OWN
STRENGTH—WE NEED THE POWER OF GOD!

That is what Paul is talking about here, being strengthened with all might, according to *God's* glorious power. In other words, walking this walk in the power of God. In the Greek text, the word for "strengthened" is in the present tense. That is, it is an ongoing activity. It is also a passive participle, not something we do for ourselves but something that is done for us. The sense here, then, is "always being strengthened." We cannot strengthen ourselves, God must do it for us. That is why Paul prays to the Lord for this.

The word for "strengthened" is *dynamis*. So is the word translated here as "might." *Dynamis* is the ability to get things done. It is, of course, where we get the word "dynamite," but don't let that fool you. It is not destructive. This power can be very constructive and life-changing in a positive way. "With all power empowered" is the literal reading here. Or as *Young's Literal Translation* puts it, "In all might being made mighty." It is a old Hebrew idiom, a Jewish way of speaking, and Paul is, after all, still very much a Jew.

With all power empowered? This can come only from God. It is "according to *His* glorious power." The word for "power" here is different than the one we saw earlier. It is *kratos*, which speaks of manifested power, power in its fullness and dominion. It is most appropriately used of God. In this passage, it speaks of "His glorious power," or the power of His glory.

Where and how has the power of His glory been manifested in all its fullness and dominion? In the creation of the heavens and the earth, certainly. But the highest, most world-changing manifestation of God's glory and power is the resurrection of Jesus the Messiah from the dead.

Therefore we were buried with Him through baptism into death, that just as Christ was raised from the dead by the glory of the Father, even so we also should walk in newness of life. (Roman 6:4)

This is the same glory and power God wants to display in you and me, not just in the *sweet by and by* but in the *here and now*, where it is so desperately needed. In his letter to the Jesus believers at Ephesus, Paul's prayer is that we may have intimate, experiential knowledge of God, to know

> *what is the exceeding greatness of His power [dynamis] toward us who believe, according to the working of His mighty power [kratos] which He worked in Christ when He raised Him from the dead and seated Him at His right hand in the heavenly places, far above all principality and power [dynamis] and might and dominion, and every name that is named, not only in this age but also in that which is to come. (Ephesians 1:19-22)*

At the end of that letter, Paul concludes,

> *Finally, my brethren, be strong [dynamis] in the Lord and in the power [kratos] of His might. (Ephesians 6:10)*

Note, again, that "be strong" (or empowered, or strengthened) is a present passive, a continuous action that happens to or in us. We are made strong "in the Lord." It is *His* power and *His* might at work. Our part is simply to yield to that work in us.

A walk worthy of the Lord is a walk made in *His* strength, always being empowered with all power by the magnificent power that manifests *His* glory and dominion—His resurrection power! It is an amazing strength—resurrection power—and it is available to every believer in Jesus. So it is possible for you and me to be always and fully strengthened with it. If it were not so then Paul, praying by the Holy Spirit, would not have prayed it.

Focus Questions

1. Why must how we live be about the power of God?

2. Why must how we live be about the glory of God?

3. How do we receive this power?

Putting Up with Joy

For all patience and longsuffering with joy. (Colossians 1:11)

Paul prays for the believers at Colosse that they will always be strengthened with all might, and he had a particular purpose in mind: "for all patience and longsuffering with joy."

The Greek word for "patience" is *hypomone*, from the word *hypomeno*, which is a compound of *hypo*, "under," and *meno*, to "stay." Figuratively, it means to undergo, to bear (as in trials), to persevere, abide, endure. Patience is the ability to persevere and endure in difficult circumstances.

In the Bible, this kind of patience is associated with hope, which is positive expectation or joyful anticipation. It is not giving up in the face of adversity or resigning yourself to it, but remaining on course, no matter what. It comes from having your expectation set on God and His promises.

The word for "longsuffering" is *macrothymia*, another compound word, from *macro*, "long," and *thymos*, passion. "Longsuffering" is the opposite of "short-tempered." We find *macrothymia* a number of times in the Septuagint (an ancient Greek translation of the Old Testament, usually noted as *LXX*). For example:

But You, O LORD, are a God full of compassion, and gracious,
Longsuffering [macrothymia] and abundant in mercy and truth.

(Psalm 86:15)

The LORD is merciful and gracious,
Slow to anger [macrothymia], and abounding in mercy.

(Psalm 103:8)

He who is slow to wrath [macrothymia] has great understanding,
But he who is impulsive exalts folly.

(Proverbs 14:29)

He who is slow to anger [macrothymia] is better than the mighty,
And he who rules his spirit than he who takes a city.

(Proverbs 16:32)

Here we can see the nature of *macrothymia*, as well as some of its benefits.

- It is the nature of God to be slow to anger.
- It flows with His compassion, mercy and grace.
- It demonstrates wisdom and creates understanding.

The one who "rules his spirit" will accomplish greater things than the one who "flies off the handle."

Patience is about persevering through difficult circumstances; longsuffering is about graciously "putting up with" difficult people. It is part of the fruit of the Spirit: Love, joy, peace, longsuffering, kindness, goodness, faithfulness, gentleness, self-control (Galatians 5:22-23). Elsewhere, Paul says,

I, therefore, the prisoner of the Lord, beseech you to walk worthy of the calling with which you were called, with all lowliness and gentleness, with longsuffering, bearing with one another in love, endeavoring to keep the unity of the Spirit in the bond of peace. (Ephesians 4:2)

Longsuffering reflects humility and gentleness. It bears with one another in love and promotes the unity of the Spirit in the bond of peace.

Enduring adversity and bearing with difficult people is hard enough by itself, but Paul adds a kicker: Do it "with joy." Now we can see why we need to be always strengthened with the power of Almighty God. Here also is why we need the promises of God and the hope (positive expectation, joyful anticipation) they bring. And this is why longsuffering comes *after* love, joy and peace when Paul lists the fruit of the Spirit. When we are filled with the love, joy and peace of God, and let them come forth in our lives, then the ability to endure adversity and bear patiently with others will follow.

Focus Questions

1. Why is hope important to being patient?

2. How does longsuffering reflect the power and glory of God?

3. How do love, joy and peace prepare us to be patient and longsuffering?

Fully Qualified for the Father's Inheritance

Giving thanks to the Father who has qualified us to be partakers
of the inheritance of the saints in the light. (Colossians 1:12)

Paul has prayed for the believers at Colosse that they may have a walk worthy of the Lord, being fully pleasing to Him in all things, bearing fruit in every good work, knowing Him more and more, being strengthened with all strength by the power of His glory, joyfully enduring difficult times and difficult people. Now he prays that they may always be giving thanks to God, the Father.

Enduring difficult circumstances. Dealing patiently with difficult people. With joy, no less. And now, always be giving thanks! Paul does not hold back in his prayer for Jesus believers. He is expecting mighty things from God. So, no matter what may be happening in our lives, no matter how thick the darkness around us may seem, there is always something much greater going on inside us by which we prevail.

First, notice to whom we are giving thanks. Not some impersonal deity, but to the *Father*. In Paul's earlier prayer, he gave thanks "to the God and Father of our Lord Jesus Christ," for the faith, hope and love at work in the Colossian believers. Now he presses in on that relationship and how it pertains to us.

The essence of fatherhood is inheritance. When we have a father, we receive a name, a family, an identity. Through faith in His son, Jesus the Messiah, we are "accepted in the Beloved" and have "obtained an inheritance" (Ephesians 1). Jesus' Father becomes our Father, His name becomes our name, His identity becomes our identity. We do not qualify ourselves for this—we cannot!—but God has done it for us, through His Son. Jesus is fully qualified and through faith, we are joined with Him. In this way, we are fully qualified in Him and can now take part in the inheritance with Him. We are "heirs of God and joint heirs with Christ" (Romans 8:17), which means that everything He inherits, we now inherit, too.

In Ephesians, Paul prayed for us to know the "riches of the glory of His inheritance in the saints" (Ephesians 1:19). "Saints in the light," is how he puts it here in Colossians. Because we are in Jesus, we are "in the light," for that is what Jesus is—light. John calls Him the "True Light" who gives light to everyone who comes into the world (John 1:9). The light shines in the darkness and the darkness cannot comprehend it, cannot overtake it, cannot put it out (John 1:5).

James, also, has something to tell us about the Father and light and inheritance. He says, "Every good gift and every perfect gift is from above, and comes down from the Father of lights, with whom there is no variation or shadow of turning" (James 1:17).

The inheritance Father has for us is nothing but good. It is full of life and light and carries with it the blessing and power of heaven. Darkness cannot overcome it, and when we learn how to walk in the reality and power of it, the will of God will be done wherever we walk on earth, just as it is in heaven.

It is a wonderful inheritance and all who entrust themselves to King Jesus the Messiah are fully qualified to take part in it. So, with David we can sing:

O LORD, You are the portion of my inheritance and my cup;
You maintain my lot.
The lines have fallen to me in pleasant places;
Yes, I have a good inheritance.

(Psalm 16:5-6)

Focus Questions

1. Why is it important to give thanks to God?

2. Why is it important that God is Father?

3. What is the inheritance God has for us?

Into the Kingdom of Light

He has delivered us from the power of darkness and conveyed us into the kingdom of the Son of His love, in whom we have redemption through His blood, the forgiveness of sins. (Colossians 1:13-14)

Paul transitions now from pastoral prayer to hymn of praise. This is what his prayer has been leading up to all along, and is what the believers at Colosse (and us, as well) desperately need to hear. He has come to the object of his passion—Jesus the Messiah, Son of God—the One through whom God has made everything possible for Paul, for the Colossians and for us. *He* is the one who is to be exalted above all because it is in *Him* that everything comes together as God has always intended.

We have been delivered—rescued!—from the "power of darkness." Jesus has done it by going through it for us. When the chief priests and the Temple guard came to arrest Him in the Garden of Gethsemane, He said, "Have you come out, as against a robber, with swords and clubs? When I was with you daily in the temple, you did not try to seize Me. But this is your hour, and the power of darkness" (Luke 22:53). On the cross, He dealt the death blow to the heart of darkness and destroyed its power from the inside out, bursting forth in glory three days later. "For this purpose the Son of God was manifested, that He might destroy the works of the devil" (1 John 3:8).

God has also "conveyed us into the kingdom of the Son of His love." The Greek word for "conveyed" was often used of the transfer or relocation of large numbers of people from one region to another, settling them as colonists or citizens. Think of how God delivered the children of Israel from out of Egypt into the Promised Land. That is the kind of picture Paul creates here. God has transferred us from out of the power of darkness and brought us into the kingdom of the Son. This is the Father's inheritance for us, as Jesus said "Do not fear, little flock, for it is your Father's good pleasure to give you the kingdom" (Luke 12:32). That is what the Father has done, He has given us the kingdom, making us a colony of heaven on earth, with Jesus as our King.

Do not think of this, though, as being removed from one kingdom into another, as if they were two equal and opposite powers. It is not like that at all. They are opposites but they are nowhere near equal. The power of darkness is no match for the kingdom of God. Darkness is not a kingdom at all. It has no rightful dominion and whatever power it did have has been broken. "The darkness is passing away, and the true light is already shining" (1 John 2:8).

God has brought us into is the kingdom of the "Son of His love" that is, His very dear and beloved Son. It was as much about God's love for the Son as it was for us, that He did this. And it was as much about the Son's love for the Father as it was for us that He came. It was their gift to each other. The love that the Father, Son and the Holy Spirit have for us is the expression, the overflow, of the love they have for each other. So when Jesus was baptized by John, the Holy Spirit descended on Him like a dove and the voice of the Father said, "This is My beloved Son, in whom I am well pleased" (Matthew 3:17). On the Mount of Transfiguration, the Father again said, "This is My beloved Son, hear Him" (Mark 9:7). We come into this kingdom, then, because we are "accepted in the Beloved" (Ephesians 1:6).

This kingdom is the kingdom of light because Jesus is the Light of the World. The light shines in the darkness and the darkness cannot overcome it (John 1:5). In Him, we are light. "We are not of the night nor of darkness" (1 Thessalonians 5:5). "For you were once darkness, but now you are light in the Lord. Walk as children of light" (Ephesians 5:8).

The kingdom God has brought us into is a kingdom of redemption where we receive the forgiveness of sins. The combination of redemption and forgiveness pictures a slave purchased at the marketplace and released from bondage. It is in Jesus that we have been redeemed out of the slave market—the price paid was His own blood. But God so loved the world that He gave the Son of His love, that whoever believes in Him should not perish but have eternal.

The Greek word for "forgiveness," refers literally to "sending away" and speaks of release from bondage. In Jesus the Messiah, the guilt of our sin is sent far away from us and we are set free to enjoy the light and life of His kingdom.

Focus Questions

1. God has conveyed us into the kingdom of the Son. Why was this necessary?

2. Could this rescue and redemption have happened apart from the Father's love for the Son or the Son's love for the Father?

3. What does life in the kingdom of the Son look like?

The Image of the Invisible

He is the image of the invisible God, the firstborn over all creation. For by Him all things were created that are in heaven and that are on earth, visible and invisible, whether thrones or dominions or principalities or powers. All things were created through Him and for Him. (Colossians 1:15-16)

Paul breaks into doxology now to sing the eternal glory and greatness of Jesus the Messiah, the Son of God's love, in whom we have redemption, the forgiveness of sins.

Jesus is the image of the invisible God. It sounds almost like a *koan,* a paradoxical saying. Like, *What is the sound of one hand clapping?* How can Jesus be the *image* of what is *invisible?*

God is invisible. He is Spirit. The material world was created by Him but it is not Him. Though the world was created to be seen, God is not subject to that condition nor is He in any way limited by our inability to see Him. It is a matter for the eyes of faith. "By faith we understand that the worlds were framed by the word of God, so that the things which are seen were not made of things which are visible" (Hebrews 11:3).

We can see *manifestations* of God's glory, but we cannot see Him in His *essence,* for He is the one who dwells "in unapproachable light, whom no man has seen or can see" (1 Timothy 6:16). But Jesus is the image of the one who is invisible. God created man in the image of God to be like Him on earth (Genesis 1:26-28), but Jesus is not only *like* God, He fully represents Him in every way. He is the "brightness of His glory, the express image of His person" (Hebrews 1:3).

Paul links the image of the invisible God with the firstborn of creation. Literally, "firstborn" speaks of one who is born first in a family. However, because the firstborn son was given the double portion inheritance, "firstborn" also came to be used to refer to the pre-eminence of one who was worthy of the highest honor.

The Son of God was not created. Indeed, He is Himself the creator of everything. "All things were made through Him, and without Him nothing was made that was made" (John 1:3). To declare this is to exalt Jesus as God, for "In the beginning, God created the heavens and the earth" (Genesis 1:1). Which was exactly the point John makes in his Gospel: "In the beginning was the Word, and the Word was with God, and the Word was God" (John 1:1). Jesus is the perfect image and expression of God because He *is* God, the creator of the heavens and the earth. John goes on to say of Him, "And the Word became flesh and dwelt among us, and we beheld His glory, the glory as of the only begotten of the Father, full of grace and truth" (John 1:14). That is why Jesus could say of Himself, "He who has seen Me has seen the Father" (John 14:9).

Paul is careful to note that Jesus is the creator of *all* things in heaven and on earth, "visible and invisible, whether thrones or dominions or principalities or powers." He alludes to the Jewish tradition of spiritual entities, established by God, that had power over the nations. The Old Testament speaks of "gods" who ruled the nations, distinct from the Most High God, Yahweh (the LORD), who ruled directly over Israel.

There was also a gnostic teaching that may have been coming around the church at Colosse, saying that there were angelic hierarchies emanating from God, the lowest of which was the architect of the material world. Such teachers considered the physical world to be flawed and therefore evil, so they denied that the Word, who is God, became flesh. Against this, Paul asserts that *all* things, the visible, material things as well as the invisible things, were created by Jesus—by Him and through Him and for Him. Therefore all fullness comes from Him and all glory belongs to Him.

Focus Questions

1. What is the relationship between the invisible and visible things of creation?

2. Why is it important that Jesus created all invisible things as well as all visible things?

3. What is the significance that all things were created *for* Him as well as *by* Him and *through* Him?

How All Things Hold Together

He is before all things, and in Him all things consist. (Colossians 1:17)

The Son of God existed before all things. "In the beginning was the Word, and the Word was with God, and the Word was God. He was in the beginning with God" (John 1:1-2). In Colossians 1:16, Paul tells us that all things were made *by* Him, *through* Him and *for* Him. "In the beginning God created the heavens and the earth," refers to the creative work of the Son. He was not created like the angelic hierarchies that were the focus of the false teachers who were trying to penetrate the community of believers at Colosse. He existed long before them. Indeed, He has always existed. He is eternal.

Paul says that in Him all things "consist." The *English Standard Version* has, "In Him all things *hold together*." The *Bible in Basic English* says, "In Him all things *have being*." By faith, we understand that the worlds were framed by the Word of God, so that the things which are visible were made by things which cannot be seen (Hebrews 11:3).

Everything is sustained in exactly the same way. The author of Hebrews speaks of the Son as being "the brightness of His [God's] glory and the express image of His person, and upholding all things by the word of His power" (Hebrews 1:3). All things were created by the word of God and are upheld by the word of God.

It is no small thing, then, that Jesus is called the Word in John 1:1, or that "the Word became flesh and dwelt among us" (John 1:14). Everything comes from the invisible word of the invisible God, and everything continues to be because of them. Jesus is the living and eternal Word who embodies and gives expression to the thoughts, desires and will of God. He is the source and sustainer of all creation.

There is mystery here: How can Jesus, born in history, be the creator of heaven and earth? Actually, this leads to a few mysteries, and the Church struggled with them for the first few centuries. First, there was how to understand the relationship between the Father, the Son and the Holy Spirit. It was mostly a question about the nature of the Lord Jesus. In AD 325, the bishops of the Church met together at Nicea and determined that the Father, Son and Spirit were one in essence and three in person. The creed that was adopted and named for this council begins:

> I believe in one God the Father almighty, Maker of heaven and earth, and of all things visible and invisible. And in one Lord Jesus Christ, the Son of God, the only-begotten, begotten of the Father before all ages; Light of Light, true God of true God, begotten, not made, of one essence with the Father, by whom all things were made. (*The Nicene Creed*, as used by the Orthodox Church in America)

But there were still questions that remained about the nature of the Son. The Church was agreed that Jesus the Son is fully divine as well as fully human. But there was disagreement about the relationship of His divinity to His humanity. In AD 451, the bishops of the Church gathered again, at Chalcedon, to address the issue. They concluded that Jesus is one person but with two natures, a fully human one as well as a fully divine one. The confession they produced begins this way:

> We, then, following the holy Fathers, all with one consent, teach men to confess one and the same Son, our Lord Jesus Christ, the same perfect in Godhead and also perfect in manhood; truly God and truly man, of a reasonable [rational] soul and body; consubstantial [co-essential] with the Father according to the Godhead, and consubstantial with us according to the Manhood. (*The Chalcedonian Definition*)

These two councils and the confessions that came from them did not so much *explain* the mysteries as *define* and *preserve* them. They did not resolve all the questions but gave the broad outline within which answers to those questions could be pursued in a way consistent with the Scriptures and the teaching of the apostles: There is but one God who exists in three persons, and the Son of God is one person with two natures.

Focus Questions

1. What is the relationship between the Word and Creation?

2. How comfortable are you about living with mystery?

3. How do we experience the mystery of who Jesus is?

The Incomparability of Divine Life

And He is the head of the body, the church, who is the beginning,
the firstborn from the dead, that in all things He may have the
preeminence. (Colossians 1:18)

Jesus, the eternal Son of God, *by* whom and *through* whom and *for* whom all things were created, and *in* whom all things hold together, is called "the head of the body." We always think of head and body together—the one implies the other. A head without a body is pointless, a body without a head is lifeless. It is quite an amazing thing, then, that Paul speaks of Jesus as "head." Equally amazing is who Paul identifies as the body of which Jesus is the head. It is the church, which is composed not of hierarchies of angels but of flesh and blood human beings, all those who belong to God through faith in Jesus. Every Jesus believer at Colosse belongs to the church and is a part of His body.

Jesus is the head of the body, the church. This speaks of vital relationship. The church is not an organization, an association that can be reduced to membership numbers and mission statements. It is an organic, living thing in which every part flows with the life of the whole. Where does this life come from? From Jesus Himself. He is not just the "head" of the body, He is the "beginning," the source, the life of the church.

Jesus is also the "firstborn from the dead." We once were dead in the rebellion of sin, Paul tells us. But in Jesus the Messiah we have been made alive.

> *But God, who is rich in mercy, because of His great love with*
> *which He loved us, even when we were dead in trespasses, made*
> *us alive together with Christ (by grace you have been saved), and*

raised us up together, and made us sit together in the heavenly places in Christ Jesus. (Ephesians 2:4-6)

In Jesus, we have spiritual life and vitality—and more. For God has raised Jesus' physical body from the dead, and that is the guarantee that all those who belong to Him, who are part of His body, will share in His resurrection life. God will raise us, too, bodily and physically from the dead.

Head, beginning, firstborn. These all speak of preeminence, and indeed, Jesus is supreme over all things, for God has

Raised Him from the dead and seated Him at His right hand in the heavenly places, far above all principality and power and might and dominion, and every name that is named, not only in this age but also in that which is to come. And He put all things under His feet, and gave Him to be head over all things to the church, which is His body, the fullness of Him who fills all in all. (Ephesians 1:20-23)

God also has highly exalted Him and given Him the name which is above every name, that at the name of Jesus every knee should bow, of those in heaven, and of those on earth, and of those under the earth, and that every tongue should confess that Jesus Christ is Lord, to the glory of God the Father. (Philippians 2:9-11)

In Colossians 1:15, Paul declared that Jesus is the "firstborn over all creation." Now, in verse 18, he calls Him "firstborn from the dead." This is the *new* creation, which has already begun with the resurrection of Jesus. In a letter to the Jesus believers at Corinth, Paul said, "Therefore, if anyone is in Christ, he is a new creation; old things have passed away; behold, all things have become new" (2 Corinthians 5:17). The new creation has begun and through faith in Jesus we become a part of it.

Jesus the Messiah is preeminent in all things, including the new creation. He is incomparable in every way and His divine life flows through us—His body, the church—now and forever.

Focus Questions

1. What is the difference between an organism and an organization?

2. Do you experience the church more as an organism or as an organization?

3. How do we experience the new, divine life we have in our head, Jesus the Messiah?

Where All Divine Fullness Dwells

For it pleased the Father that in Him all the fullness should dwell. (Colossians 1:19)

The word "for" introduces a reason or purpose. Here, Paul explains why God has done what He has in regard to the Son.

- ❧ Why Jesus has come as the express image of the invisible God
- ❧ Why He has been given supremacy over all creation
- ❧ Why all things have been made by Him, through Him and for Him
- ❧ Why all things hold together in Him
- ❧ Why He is the head of the body (the church), the beginning, and the firstborn from the dead
- ❧ Why He has the preeminence in all things

It was because it pleased the Father that in Him all fullness should dwell!

Now, the words "the Father" are not in the Greek text, but the idea of God is certainly implied by the context. Different translations handle this in various ways. For example:

- "For in him all the fullness of God was pleased to dwell." (*English Standard Version*)
- "Because in him it did please all the fullness to tabernacle." (*Young's Literal Translation*)
- "For God in full measure was pleased to be in him." (*Bible in Basic English*)
- "Because in Him [God] was well pleased that all the fullness be permanently at home." (Wuest's *Expanded Translation*)
- "Because all the fullness of God was pleased to live in Him." (*Common English Bible*)

The point is that all the fullness of the divine nature dwells in the Son. The "fullness" Paul is talking about is every attribute and power that belongs to God. The Greek word for "fullness" is *pleroma*. Paul appears to be using this particular word in order to counter the false teachers who were trying to get into the church at Colosse.

Pleroma was the central term of the gnostics, who used it to refer to God. But they believed that creation was separated from God by numerous demigods, angelic hierarchies or other intermediaries. Some intermediaries might possess this or that power while others might have various other divine attributes. But only God, who in their view was very distant, possessed every divine power and attribute.

Paul, however, delivers a stunning blow to this doctrine. The *Pleroma*, the fullness of all the divine attributes and powers, is *not* far, far away, separated from us by layers and levels of entities and emanations. But it has come very close to us—as close as human skin—in the person of Jesus the Messiah, the Son of God who became flesh and dwelt among us.

Paul delivers this knockout punch again in Colossians 2:9: "For in Him dwells all the fullness of the Godhead bodily" (we will talk about this more as we continue through Paul's letter). The material creation is not evil, nor is the physical body, as the gnostics supposed. But God considered it quite appropriate that the divine essence, with all the attributes and powers of God, should reside in the human flesh of the Son, Jesus the Messiah, and dwell among us in the world.

Focus Questions

1. Why do you suppose it pleased the Father that all fullness should dwell in the God-man, Jesus the Messiah?

2. What does this say about the created universe?

3. What does this say about humankind?

Reconciling Heaven and Earth

For it pleased the Father that in Him all the fullness should dwell, and by Him to reconcile all things to Himself, by Him, whether things on earth or things in heaven, having made peace through the blood of His cross. (Colossians 1:19-20)

It pleased the Father that all the divine essence, power and attributes reside in Jesus the Messiah. But it also pleased God that all things in heaven and earth be reconciled by the Son. These are not two unrelated statements but belong together in a very important way. It was necessary that the fullness of God abide in the Son in order for all things in heaven and earth to be reconciled by Him. Because all things in heaven and earth were created *by* Him and *for* Him, and *in* Him all things hold together. This is, indeed, what makes it even *possible* for all things in heaven and earth to be reconciled.

Paul speaks about this reconciliation in his other letters, although a bit differently. God's plan, he says, is that "in the dispensation of the fullness of the times He might gather together in one all things in Christ, both which are in heaven and which are on earth—in Him" (Ephesians 1:10).

> *Therefore God also has highly exalted Him and given Him the name which is above every name, that at the name of Jesus every knee should bow, of those in heaven, and of those on earth, and of those under the earth, and that every tongue should confess that Jesus Christ is Lord, to the glory of God the Father" (Philippians 2:9-11)*

Let's go back to the beginning for a moment, when God made the heavens and the earth in Genesis 1. At the end of that chapter we read, "Then God saw everything that He had made, and indeed it was very good" (Genesis 1:31). The physical creation was not evil, as the gnostics supposed, but was very good. However, it fell away from the blessing of God because Adam, who was made from the dust of the earth (as well as the breath of God) and given dominion over it, rebelled against God.

This is why Jesus came, to set things right in the world. For the Gnostics, this simply was not possible because of their belief that the material world is not merely fallen but inherently evil. The amazing thing, though, is that Jesus has not only reconciled heaven and earth but He did it in a very physical way: through the blood of His cross. The wood of the cross and the nails that pierced Him were real and tangible. So was the flesh of His body and the blood that He shed. By these material realities, He has reconciled heaven and earth and made peace between God and humankind.

The emphasis here is on the Son. It is in *Him*, not through angelic intermediaries, that God has done this. It was through the shedding of *His* blood. Angels could not bring about reconciliation because they are not of earth. But the Son of God is of both heaven *and* earth, being fully divine and fully human. He is of heaven because He is the creator of all; He is of earth because He "became flesh and dwelt among us" (John 1:14). Jesus is the only one in the universe able to bring heaven and earth together—and He has done it through His own body and blood, and the crudeness of the cross.

The work necessary for reconciliation has already been accomplished. We live now in the time when the benefits of that work are being increasingly revealed in the world, especially in humankind.

> *For the earnest expectation of the creation eagerly waits for the revealing of the sons of God. For the creation was subjected to futility, not willingly, but because of Him who subjected it in hope; because the creation itself also will be delivered from the bondage of corruption into the glorious liberty of the children of God. For we know that the whole creation groans and labors with birth pangs together until now. (Romans 8:19-22)*

In the end, heaven and earth will be joined together, with the kingdom of God fully come and the will of God done on earth exactly as it is in heaven. We read about this in Revelation 21. In the meantime, "the darkness is passing away, and the true light is already shining" (1 John 2:8).

Focus Questions

1. Does it surprise you that all the issues of the universe, including the spiritual ones, could be resolved by flesh and blood, and the tangibility of the cross?

2. What do you suppose it means that everything in heaven and on earth will be reconciled?

3. In view of this, what do you believe awaits you after this life?

The Gospel of God's Pleasure

For it pleased the Father that in Him all the fullness should dwell, and by Him to reconcile all things to Himself, by Him, whether things on earth or things in heaven, having made peace through the blood of His cross. (Colossians 1:19-20)

The good news of the gospel is that it pleased the Father that all the fullness of divinity should dwell in Jesus the Son, the Word who became flesh and dwelt among us (John 1:14).

The good news of the gospel is that it pleased God to reconcile all things in heaven and on earth to Himself. When Jesus came, He announced that the kingdom of heaven, a.k.a, the kingdom of God, was now at hand—present on earth. All His works on earth were a demonstration of the authority and power of the kingdom, and He taught the disciples to pray, "Kingdom of God, come! Will of God, be done on earth as it is in heaven!" (Matthew 6:10 *JVD*).

The good news of the gospel is that it pleased God to make peace—*shalom*, wholeness, oneness—through the violence of Jesus' blood shed on the cross. There the battle was fought and there the victory was won.

The good news of the gospel is that it pleased God that those who were once alienated from Him, whose thoughts and works were against Him, should now be reconciled to Him in the flesh-and-blood body of Jesus. It pleased God that through Jesus' death on the cross, we should be presented holy, blameless and above reproach before Him, now and at the last day.

The good news of the gospel is that it pleased God that we should participate in this reconciliation, not by the futility of human striving, but purely through faith in Jesus, in whom all the fullness of God dwells in human flesh. This is the "hope" of the gospel, the positive expectation and joyful anticipation of what God has for us, in this life and the next.

The gospel of God's pleasure presents us with this good news, this hope, this expectation: The wholeness of God's *shalom* in the world—the reconciliation of heaven and earth, of God and humanity, through faith in King Jesus the Messiah.

Focus Questions

1. How big are the needs of the world?

2. How big are the parameters of the gospel?

3. How big is the pleasure of God?

Once Alienated, Now Unaccusable

And you, who once were alienated and enemies in your mind by wicked works, yet now He has reconciled in the body of His flesh through death, to present you holy, and blameless, and above reproach in His sight. (Colossians 1:21-23)

In Jesus the Messiah heaven and earth are reconciled and peace has been made between God and humankind through the blood of His cross. Paul now shows how this works.

We once were alienated from God. This estrangement resulted in broken relationships—with creation, each other, even within our own selves. We were out of joint with earth as well as heaven. We were "enemies" (the Greek word means "hateful") towards God. Our thoughts and imaginations about God were hostile and revealed themselves through bitter, hostile deeds.

"Yet now," Paul says. What wonderful words those are! What Paul just described about alienation and enemies was *before*. But *now* everything has changed because Jesus has reconciled us, brought us back into proper relationship with God. That makes all the difference in the world because now we have full access into the presence of God. Jesus has done this through His own flesh-and-blood body. Paul emphasizes this once more because false teachers died not believe that the Son of God even had a physical body, much less that any reconciliation could have been accomplished through it.

God was pleased to reconcile us through the cross of Jesus the Messiah so that He could "present" us holy, blameless and above reproach in His sight. The Greek verb for "present" is in the aorist tense, signifying completed action, a "done deal." To be holy means to be consecrated, set apart for God and God alone. "Without blame" picks up the idea of a spotless offering, without blemish. "Above reproach" (not just *without* reproach but *above* reproach) means that no charge can now be laid against us.

But how can this be, for who among us has lived blamelessly and above reproach? Yet, Jesus presents us this way before the Father. He alone was without sin and spotless, and He offered Himself as a sacrifice for our sake, making peace through His death on the cross. He Himself is the sacrifice presented before the Father, and it is as we are *in Him*, through faith in Him, that *we* also are presented before God as holy and blameless and above reproach. That is how God sees us now as well as how He will see on us on the final day when we stand before Him.

> *Blessed be the God and Father of our Lord Jesus Christ, who has blessed us with every spiritual blessing in the heavenly places in Christ, just as He chose us in Him before the foundation of the world, that we should be holy and without blame before Him in love. (Ephesians 1:3-4)*

> *Just as Christ also loved the church and gave Himself for her, that He might sanctify and cleanse her with the washing of water by the word, that He might present her to Himself a glorious church, not having spot or wrinkle or any such thing, but that she should be holy and without blemish. (Ephesians 5:25-27)*

The devil is an accuser. In fact, that is what *diabolos*, the Greek word for "devil," actually means, *accuser* or *slanderer*. In the book of Revelation he is called, "the accuser of our brethren." However, there is now no accusation he can make that can stand against us. Ever.

Who shall bring a charge against God's elect? It is God who justifies. Who is he who condemns? It is Christ who died, and furthermore is also risen, who is even at the right hand of God, who also makes intercession for us. Who shall separate us from the love of Christ? ... For I am persuaded that neither death nor life, nor angels nor principalities nor powers, nor things present nor things to come, nor height nor depth, nor any other created thing, shall be able to separate us from the love of God which is in Christ Jesus our Lord. (Romans 8:33-35, 38-39)

Now salvation, and strength, and the kingdom of our God, and the power of His Christ have come, for the accuser of our brethren, who accused them before our God day and night, has been cast down. (Revelation 12:10)

Focus Questions

1. Where do you locate yourself in God's plan for reconciliation, with regard to your relationship with God, creation, others and yourself?

2. Jesus has presented us holy and blameless before the Father. What confidence does that give you concerning your relationship with God?

3. We often do not *experience* ourselves as being holy and blameless. What will you answer when the voice of the accuser whispers in your ear?

Continue in the Faith

... if indeed you continue in the faith, grounded and steadfast, and are not moved away from the hope of the gospel which you heard, which was preached to every creature under heaven, of which I, Paul, became a minister. (Colossians 1:23)

It is the Father's good will to reconcile all things in heaven and earth through the Son, by the shedding of His blood on the cross. This is the good news of the gospel. We participate in this reconciliation by believing the gospel of Jesus the Messiah. This was the good news the believers at Colosse first heard from Epaphras, who learned it from Paul. This gospel, then, is the one Paul himself ministered and which, even in his day, had gone out into all the world.

"If indeed you continue in the faith." They had already begun in the faith and were "grounded and steadfast" in it (Paul gave thanks for that earlier). The Greek words picture a building properly settled on a good foundation. Paul does not want them to be "moved away" or shifted off the foundation that has been laid for them, the "hope of the gospel." Hope is not about uncertainty but about expectation. Their expectation was seated on a good foundation, the gospel. There is only one gospel, and it is preached to everyone in the world, not just to an elite group as the false teachers would have it. And there is only one foundation upon which we can properly be established. But care must be taken about what is built upon it. That is what Paul is zealous to protect. He addressed this in his letter to the Jesus believers at Corinth.

According to the grace of God which was given to me, as a wise master builder I have laid the foundation, and another builds on it. But let each one take heed how he builds on it. For no other foundation can anyone lay than that which is laid, which is Jesus Christ. Now if anyone builds on this foundation with gold, silver, precious stones, wood, hay, straw, each one's work will become clear; for the Day will declare it, because it will be revealed by fire; and the fire will test each one's work, of what sort it is. (1 Corinthians 3:10-13)

Now Paul wants them to *continue* in the faith in which they began, and indeed, he is confident that they will (the use of "if" here is rhetorical). That is exactly why he writes. He sees false teaching coming in on them and he wants to preempt it and prevent it from gaining any foothold so that they remain firm in their faith in Jesus and the wonderful expectation that comes from the gospel.

Now, therefore, you are no longer strangers and foreigners, but fellow citizens with the saints and members of the household of God, having been built on the foundation of the apostles and prophets, Jesus Christ Himself being the chief cornerstone, in whom the whole building, being fitted together, grows into a holy temple in the Lord, in whom you also are being built together for a dwelling place of God in the Spirit. (Ephesians 2:19-22)

The good news of Jesus the Messiah is about the reconciliation of heaven and earth and is the foundation of every good expectation for those who continue in their faith in Him.

Focus Questions

1.   Why is it important to continue in the faith?

2. What is God's part in this?

3. What is our part?

Filling Up the Afflictions of Messiah

I now rejoice in my sufferings for you, and fill up in my flesh what is lacking in the afflictions of Christ, for the sake of His body, which is the church. (Colossians 1:24)

Paul endured many afflictions for the sake of the gospel. "I ... fill up," he says. The Greek verb behind it is based on the word *pleroo*. That was a favorite word for the gnostic teachers and it seems Paul never misses an opportunity in this letter to relate all fullness to the Lord Jesus in one way or another. "In my flesh," he says, again affirming the physical, *this world* nature of the gospel (against the false teaching that matter is inherently evil). Jesus the Messiah has a body, a physical presence in the world. The church is that body and Paul is part of the church, so when he is persecuted, the church suffers affliction, and when the church suffers affliction, Jesus suffers affliction in His body. In one of his letters to the believers at Corinth, Paul details some of the persecutions he experienced.

In labors more abundant, in stripes above measure, in prisons more frequently, in deaths often. From the Jews five times I received forty stripes minus one. Three times I was beaten with rods; once I was stoned; three times I was shipwrecked; a night and a day I have been in the deep; in journeys often, in perils of waters, in perils of robbers, in perils of my own countrymen, in perils of the Gentiles, in perils in the city, in perils in the wilderness, in perils in the sea, in perils among false brethren; in weariness and toil, in sleeplessness often, in hunger and thirst, in fastings often, in cold and nakedness—besides the other things, what comes upon me daily: my deep concern for all the churches. (2 Corinthians 11:23-28)

This came as no surprise. When Paul (then known as Saul) was headed to Damascus to persecute the believers there, the Lord Jesus stopped him in his tracks. A bright light suddenly shone all around and a voice said, "Saul, Saul, why are you persecuting me?" "Who are you, Lord?" Saul asked. "I am Jesus, whom you are persecuting" (Acts 9:4-5). So Paul understood that the persecution of Christians is the persecution of Jesus Himself.

Saul became a believer in Jesus as the Messiah that day and was literally blinded by the experience. So God spoke to another man, Ananias, to go and lay hands on him to restore his sight. Ananias was reluctant; it was still only very recently that Saul had been persecuting believers. But the Lord Jesus said, "Go, for he is a chosen vessel of Mine to bear My name before Gentiles, kings, and the children of Israel. *For I will show him how many things he must suffer for My name's sake*" (Acts 9:15-16). Paul was very aware that he would be persecuted for preaching about Jesus.

So when Paul speaks of "filling up" what was lacking in the "afflictions of Christ," he is not referring to the passion of the cross and the work of atonement Jesus did for us there—that work was full and complete! He is talking about being persecuted for the sake of Jesus and the gospel. Paul suffered many afflictions as did the other apostles because of the gospel message they preached. In Acts 5 we read about Peter and the apostles when they were arrested and put in jail. The authorities were so enraged they wanted to kill them but released them instead, warning them not to preach about Jesus anymore. "So they departed from the presence of the council, rejoicing that they were counted worthy to suffer shame for His name. And daily in the temple, and in every house, they did not cease teaching and preaching Jesus as the Christ" (Acts 5:41-42). Paul and the other apostles did not just put up with these afflictions, they rejoiced in them. He explains why in his letter to the Jesus believers at Philippi, written from a prison cell (as is this letter to the believers at Colosse).

> *But I want you to know, brethren, that the things which happened to me have actually turned out for the furtherance of the gospel, so that it has become evident to the whole palace guard, and to all the rest, that my chains are in Christ; and most of the brethren in the Lord, having become confident by my chains, are much more bold to speak the word without fear.*
>
> *Some indeed preach Christ even from envy and strife, and some also from goodwill: The former preach Christ from selfish ambition, not sincerely, supposing to add affliction to my chains; but the latter out of love, knowing that I am appointed for the defense of the gospel. What then? Only that in every way, whether in pretense or in truth, Christ is preached; and in this I rejoice, yes, and will rejoice. (Philippians 1:12-18)*

Persecution for the sake of the gospel has persisted throughout the history of the Church. Even today, there are many Christians around the world who are being cruelly treated and martyred for their faith in Jesus (for example, visit The Voice of the Martyrs at *www.persecution.com*). These too are "filling up" the "afflictions of Christ." Yet, surprisingly—and supernaturally—they rejoice! Because the Lord

Jesus is glorified in their physical bodies, whether by life or by death, He is with them always.

But now notice how this comes around full circle. Paul, when he was called Saul, once persecuted Christians because of their faith. Then he came to understand that in persecuting the church, he was actually persecuting Messiah. Turning to the Lord Jesus on the way to Damascus, he was then willing to suffer persecution for His sake. And now he rejoices because he understands that all the persecutions he endures because of Jesus and the gospel is for the sake of His body, the church.

Focus Questions

1. What do you think of when you think of persecution?

2. How was Paul, and how are Christians who are being persecuted today, able to rejoice in their sufferings?

3. How does this benefit the church, the body of Messiah?

Stewards of Divine Mysteries

… of which I became a minister according to the stewardship from God which was given to me for you, to fulfill the word of God, the mystery which has been hidden from ages and from generations, but now has been revealed to His saints. (Colossians 1:25-26)

"Of which" refers to the Church, the body of Jesus the Messiah. Paul identifies himself as a minister—a servant—of the Church. The sufferings he spoke of in verse 24 were for the sake of the Church.

The Focus of Our Faith ~ Paul's Letter to the Jesus Believers at Colosse

The stewardship he speaks of now is also for the sake of the Church. Stewardship is a responsibility to administer properly what has been committed to the steward. The stewardship Paul has in mind here was from God, "given to me for you." God gave Paul the responsibility of administering the Word of God properly to His people, to "fulfill" it (there's that word *pleroo* again). Paul further identifies the Word of God, and its fulfillment, in terms of "mystery." It is one of his favorite words. He uses it seventeen times in his letters, including four times in this one.

The stewardship Paul received from God concerns divine mysteries. "Let a man so consider us, as servants of Christ and stewards of the mysteries of God" (1 Corinthians 4:1). In the Bible, a mystery is a divine secret, to be revealed at the appropriate time. God hinted at them in the Old Testament. "The secret things belong to the Lord our God, but those things which are revealed belong to us and to our children forever" (Deuteronomy 29:29). The Lord Jesus reveals them in the New. "All these things Jesus spoke to the multitude in parables; and without a parable He did not speak to them, that it might be fulfilled which was spoken by the prophet, saying: 'I will open My mouth in parables; I will utter things kept secret from the foundation of the world'" (Matthew 13:34-35).

Gnostic religion had its mysteries, too, secret teachings that were not given to all but were revealed only as one progressed to a certain level of knowledge. For Paul, however, the mysteries of which he was given stewardship were secrets that, though they at one time had been hidden, were now being revealed to *every* believer. His stewardship was to "fulfill the word of God," that is, to preach the mysteries that God has now revealed in Jesus the Messiah. Look at how Paul describes some of these mysteries.

> ～ "We speak the wisdom of God in a *mystery*, the hidden wisdom which God ordained before the ages for our glory, which none of

the rulers of this age knew; for had they known, they would not have crucified the Lord of glory." (1 Corinthians 2:7-8)

- "Having made known to us the *mystery* of His will, according to His good pleasure which He purposed in Himself, that in the dispensation of the fullness of the times He might gather together in one all things in Christ, both which are in heaven and which are on earth—in Him." (Ephesians 1:9-10)

- "By revelation He made known to me the *mystery* ... which in other ages was not made known to the sons of men, as it has now been revealed by the Spirit to His holy apostles and prophets: that the Gentiles should be fellow heirs, of the same body, and partakers of His promise in Christ through the gospel." (Ephesians 3:3-6)

- "To me, who am less than the least of all the saints, this grace was given, that I should preach among the Gentiles the unsearchable riches of Christ, and to make all see what is the fellowship of the *mystery*, which from the beginning of the ages has been hidden in God who created all things through Jesus Christ." (Ephesians 3:8-9)

- "We are members of His body, of His flesh and of His bones ... This is a great *mystery*, but I speak concerning Christ and the church." (Ephesians 5:30-32)

- "[Pray] for me, that utterance may be given to me, that I may open my mouth boldly to make known the *mystery* of the gospel." (Ephesians 6:19)

- "And without controversy great is the *mystery* of godliness: God was manifested in the flesh, justified in the Spirit, seen by angels, preached among the Gentiles, believed on in the world, received up in glory." (1 Timothy 3:16)

- "Behold, I tell you a *mystery*: We shall not all sleep, but we shall all be changed." (1 Corinthians 15:51)

These divine mysteries reveal to every believer how God is redeeming the world through Jesus the Messiah.

Focus Questions

1. Why did God keep these things hidden in Old Testament times?

2. Why have they been revealed to us in the New Testament?

3. Now that they have been revealed to us, what and to whom is our stewardship responsibility?

The Revelation of Divine Glory in You

> *To them God willed to make known what are the riches of the glory of this mystery among the Gentiles: which is Christ in you, the hope of glory. (Colossians 1:27)*

Paul is caught up in the richness of the glorious mystery that has been given him by God to make known to everyone who believes in Jesus, to the "saints" (who are set apart as God's own). The mystery is that the revelation of the riches and glory of God was not just for believing Jews, who had an expectation that Messiah would come to deliver them and fulfill God's purpose for Israel. But it was also for—and this was a surprise—believing Gentiles as well. Paul fleshes that out some in his letter to the believers at Ephesus.

> *Therefore remember that you, once Gentiles in the flesh—who are called Uncircumcision by what is called the Circumcision made*

in the flesh by hands—that at that time you were without Christ, being aliens from the commonwealth of Israel and strangers from the covenants of promise, having no hope and without God in the world. But now in Christ Jesus you who once were far off have been brought near by the blood of Christ. (Ephesians 2:11-13)

This is the mystery "which in other ages was not made known to the sons of men, as it has now been revealed by the Spirit to His holy apostles and prophets: that the Gentiles should be fellow heirs, of the same body, and partakers of His promise in Christ through the gospel" (Ephesians 3:5-6). Peter speaks similarly of those who "once were not a people but are now the people of God, who had not obtained mercy but now have obtained mercy" (1 Peter 2:10).

The mystery of which Paul now speaks is not merely that we are all named together as the people of Jesus the Messiah. It is not even that He dwells *among* us. But the rich glory in which Paul revels is that Jesus, God's Messiah, dwells *in* us! "Christ *in* you, the hope of glory." Once upon a time, we had come short of the glory of God because of our sinfulness (Romans 3:23). But Jesus has dealt with our sin and now the glory of God resides in us—Jesus now lives His life in us by the Holy Spirit. Paul says,

I have been crucified with Christ; it is no longer I who live, but Christ lives in me; and the life which I now live in the flesh I live by faith in the Son of God, who loved me and gave Himself for me. (Galatians 2:20)

You are not in the flesh but in the Spirit, if indeed the Spirit of God dwells in you. Now if anyone does not have the Spirit of Christ, he is not His. (Romans 8:9)

This is the mystery that has been revealed: All the fullness of God dwells in Jesus, and Jesus dwells in us. In this, we find the "hope of glory," the joyful anticipation of every good thing in God being revealed in us—spirit, soul and body. The apostle Peter speaks of the same thing in this way:

> *His divine power has given to us all things that pertain to life and godliness, through the knowledge of Him who called us by glory and virtue, by which have been given to us exceedingly great and precious promises, that through these you may be partakers of the divine nature. (1 Peter 1:3-4)*

The apostle John said it like this: "Beloved, now we are children of God; and it has not yet been revealed what we shall be, but we know that when He is revealed, we shall be like Him, for we shall see Him as He is. And everyone who has this hope in Him purifies himself, just as He is pure" (1 John 3:2-3).

It is in Jesus, not in any angelic order, that we have this joyful expectation and partake of the divine nature. As we begin to live in anticipation of His divine life being made fully known in us, we find that we are changed here and now.

Focus Questions

1. Why does Paul speak particularly of this mystery being revealed to the Gentiles?

2. How is the glory of God revealed in Jesus the Messiah?

3. How is the glory of Jesus the Messiah revealed in you?

Presenting Everyone Perfect

Him we preach, warning every man and teaching every man in all wisdom, that we may present every man perfect in Christ Jesus. (Colossians 1:28)

The first thing to note here is that "Him" is in the emphatic position. It emphasizes *Jesus* as the content of Paul's preaching. Not the worship of angels, principalities, powers and dominions that was promoted by the false teachers. The Greek word for "preach" means to declare or proclaim. Paul proclaims Jesus above all else because only in Him does all the fullness of God dwell, only through Him were all things created, only in Him do all things hold together, and only by Him are all things in heaven and earth reconciled.

Paul's preaching is all about Jesus the Messiah and by it he constantly "warns" (admonishes or exhorts) and teaches everyone. Exhortation calls for action or response, which in this case is about remaining solidly in the faith, keeping the focus firmly on the Lord Jesus. Teaching has to do with instruction concerning the content of faith, the truth about who Jesus is and what that means in regard to God's plan for the world.

Notice that Paul says "every man" three times (the Greek refers to every human being, whether male or female). This, too, is emphatic. He exhorts *every person* and teaches *every person* so that he might present *every person* perfect in Jesus. Gnostic teaching was not intended for everyone, only for those who attained a certain level of understanding. But Paul's gospel is for all. Everyone counts, and he does not want anyone to get left behind.

Paul exhorts and teaches everyone "in all wisdom." This is not the wisdom of the world, nor the wisdom of the gnostics, whose secret teachings were limited only to some. It is the wisdom of God.

Where is the wise? Where is the scribe? Where is the disputer of this age? Has not God made foolish the wisdom of this world? For since, in the wisdom of God, the world through wisdom did not know God, it pleased God through the foolishness of the message preached to save those who believe. For Jews request a sign, and Greeks seek after wisdom; but we preach Christ crucified, to the Jews a stumbling block and to the Greeks foolishness, but to those who are called, both Jews and Greeks, Christ the power of God and the wisdom of God. (1 Corinthians 1:20-24)

The wisdom of God is available to everyone in Jesus the Messiah. "But of Him you are in Christ Jesus, who became for us wisdom from God" (1 Corinthians 1:30). Nothing is held back, for in Jesus the Messiah "are hidden all the treasures of wisdom and knowledge" (Colossians 2:3).

In Colossians 1:22, Paul spoke of how Jesus came to present us holy, blameless and above reproach in the eyes of the Father. In verse 28, Paul desires to present everyone perfect in Jesus, through faith in the gospel. The Greek verb for "present" in both verses is in the aorist tense, which speaks of completed action, as distinct from ongoing or progressive action. Jesus does not have to present us over and over again as holy and blameless before God. Once He has presented us, it is a done deal. Likewise, Paul does not seek to present everyone over and over in Jesus, but to present everyone in such a way that has enduring effect, through faith in Jesus.

The Greek word for "perfect" is *teleios* and refers to what is mature and complete, fulfilling the purpose for which it was made. Here again, Paul counters error without even mentioning it by name, simply by teaching the truth. *Teleios* was another word used by the gnostic teachers, but only of those who attained complete understanding of their doctrine; it was a perfection only a few would attain. But Paul preaches the gospel of Jesus the Messiah to *everyone*, exhorting and teaching *everyone* about Him—focusing everyone on Him—that *everyone* might be found mature and complete in Him on judgment day.

Focus Questions

1. Do you believe it is possible for Jesus to be the focus of everything you do?

2. Do you believe it is practical and productive for Jesus to be the focus of everything you do?

3. What hinders you from letting Jesus be the focus of everything you do?

His Energy Energizing Me

To this end I also labor, striving according to His working which works in me mightily. (Colossians 1:29)

Paul's purpose in preaching the good news about Jesus is to present everyone mature and complete in Him. Everything in Paul is focused on that goal. This little verse is loaded with the power by which he goes about that work. "To this end I also *labor, striving* according to His *working* which *works* in me *mightily*."

- ~ The Greek word for "labor" means to toil to the point of fatigue.
- ~ The word for "striving" is *agonizomai*, which is where we get our

English word "agony." We often think of it as intense pain, but Paul is actually talking about an intense effort.

❧ The word for "working" is *energeia*, from which we get the English word "energy." It is the ability or strength to operate efficiently and get things done.

❧ The word for "work" is the verb form, *energeo*.

❧ The word "mightily" actually translates two words that are more literally rendered as "in power." The Greek word for power is *dynamis*. When Paul uses it, it is almost always about supernatural power and usually about the miraculous power of God.

Paul labors hard and puts forth great effort for the sake of Jesus and the Church. Yet, it is not his energy that does the work. His whole life now is about Jesus the Messiah and the life of Messiah living in him. He is energized with the energy of Jesus! "I have been crucified with Christ; it is no longer I who live, but Christ lives in me" (Galatians 2:20). This energy is the supernatural power of God at work in and through him to accomplish mighty things, which he could never have hoped to do on his own. His whole ministry is a display of God's mighty power at work through Jesus the Messiah.

And my speech and my preaching were not with persuasive words of human wisdom, but in demonstration of the Spirit and of power, that your faith should not be in the wisdom of men but in the power of God. (1 Corinthians 2:4-5)

For the kingdom of God is not in word but in power. (1 Corinthians 4:19-20)

The energy that works in Paul so powerfully is not just for him but is available to every believer in Jesus. For it is *His* power, the power by which He did so many miraculous things. Indeed, it is the power that raised Him from the dead and seated Him at the right hand of the Father (Ephesians 1:19-22). It is the power of the Holy Spirit, which He promised to the Church at Pentecost (Acts 1:8). Earlier, Paul prayed for the believers at Colosse that they would be "strengthened with all might," according to this glorious power" (Colossians 1:11). It is that power of Jesus living in them—and us!—as well as in Paul.

Now to Him who is able to do exceedingly abundantly above all that we ask or think, according to [His] power that works in us, to Him be glory in the church by Christ Jesus to all generations, forever and ever. Amen. (Ephesians 3:20-21)

Focus Questions

1. What is the relationship between our effort and God's energy?

2. How does the power of God reveal the Lord Jesus?

3. What might this power look like in your life?

Hidden Treasures of Wisdom and Knowledge

For I want you to know what a great conflict I have for you and those in Laodicea, and for as many as have not seen my face in the flesh, that their hearts may be encouraged, being knit together in love, and attaining to all riches of the full assurance of understanding, to the knowledge of the mystery of God, both

> *of the Father and of Christ, in whom are hidden all the treasures of wisdom and knowledge. (Colossians 2:1-3)**

Paul had an intense concern for the Jesus believers at Colosse and Laodicea and the entire region. They had been targeted by gnostic teachers who promoted a "secret" wisdom and knowledge to which only a few attained. Paul was determined to protect them from this error. Not that he did not want them to have wisdom and knowledge—he very much desired that they should experience the "mystery" of God it in all its fullness. But the gnostics taught that God was a distant deity whose fullness was too pure for the material realm and was separated from us by a hierarchy of angelic beings.

"As many as have not seen my face in the flesh." It almost seems like Paul says this as a dig against the false teachers. For the gnostics, only the spiritual realm was good; the material world was not merely corrupt but was inherently evil. So Paul gets in their face, so to speak, with reference to material things: his face and his flesh. Ha!

Paul wanted the believers at Colosse to "know" (Greek, *eido*, to "see" or "perceive") what "conflict" (Greek, *agon*, from which we get "agony") he was going through on their behalf. This was a serious matter and he was engaged in a magnificent purpose. Let's look at how various translations have put it:

> *In order that their hearts may be cheered, they themselves being welded together in love and enjoying all the advantages of a reasonable certainty, till at last they attain the full knowledge of God's truth, which is Christ Himself. (Weymouth New Testament)*

---

* The *NKJV* adds "both of the Father and," but there is no basis for this in the earliest Greek manuscripts of the New Testament.

How I long that you may be encouraged, and find out more and more how strong are the bonds of Christian love. How I long for you to grow more certain in your knowledge and more sure in your grasp of God himself. May your spiritual experience become richer as you see more and more fully God's great secret, Christ himself! (J. B. Phillips, The New Testament in Modern English)

Know that I'm on your side, right alongside you. You're not in this alone. I want you woven into a tapestry of love, in touch with everything there is to know of God. Then you will have minds confident and at rest, focused on Christ, God's Great mystery. (The Message)

There is one purpose here but with three facets:

- That they may be encouraged, comforted, cheered because they are not alone but have each other.
- That they may be knit together, woven together, bonded together, welded together in love.
- That they may have a full, rich "knowledge" (Greek, *epignosis*) of God, that is, to know Him not just in theory but in experience.

There is a great confidence, a "full assurance" that comes with this. The Greek word is *plerophoria*, a compound of *pleres* and *phoreo*. *Pleres* means replete, complete or full. It is where the word *pleroma*, "fullness," comes from. Once again, Paul is bringing a buzzword of the false teachers into the service of the Lord Jesus. *Phoreo* means to bring or bear. Paul desires that through their love for one another they may come to "bear the fullness" of understanding in knowing God.

This full, rich, experiential knowledge of the Father comes to us in Jesus the Messiah, who is the "mystery" of God. For the gnostics, divine mystery was a secret knowledge revealed only to a few. But for Paul, the mystery of God was something that was once hidden but is now revealed to *everyone* through the Lord Jesus. In Him, all that is true and all that is wise comes to light. We will see more of how that happens in the next section.

Paul's emphasis is ever and always on Jesus. It is in Him—not in the esoterica and angelic hierarchies of the false teachers but in Jesus alone—that we find all the treasures of wisdom and knowledge and come to experience, with confident assurance, the fullness of knowing God.

Focus Questions

1. What encouragement comes in knowing that we have each other?

2. How does being woven together with each other in love help us know God more fully?

3. Why is it not enough to simply have information *about* God?

Woven Together in Love

I want you woven into a tapestry of love, in touch with everything there is to know of God. Then you will have minds confident and at rest, focused on Christ, God's Great mystery. (Colossians 2:2 The Message)

Paul has an intense desire and concern that the Jesus believers at Colosse be "woven together into a tapestry of love." This is because he wants them to know and experience, in a very intimate way, the revelation of God in Jesus the Messiah—and the one does not come without the other. Until we are bound to each other in love, we will not really know or understand God because love is *of* God and indeed God *is* love (1 John 4:7-8).

God Himself is "woven together" in love. The early Church Fathers had a special word to describe the relationship of Father, Son and Holy Spirit: *perichoresis*. It is a Greek word made up of two parts: *peri*, which means "around," and *choresis*, from which we get the word "choreography." It was used to describe the interaction, the interrelationship, the *divine dance* of the three persons of the Godhead. Love in love with love.

The mystery of God, which is not hidden away for a select few but is made available to all, is revealed to us in Jesus the Messiah by the Holy Spirit. Divine love throughout. God so loved the world that He gave His Son (John 3:16). "Greater love has no one than this, than to lay down one's life for his friends," Jesus said—and then He did just that. And of course Paul tells us, "the fruit of the Spirit is love" (Galatians 5:22).

If we would know and experience and enjoy and dwell in this mystery, we must enter into a life of love for each other. Understand, though, that this love is not something we must work up on our own. We cannot. But it comes to us as a gift from God, who *is* love, and who is the giver of all good gifts. Our part is to yield to it and let it work in us and through us. As we submit to divine love, God will weave us into a rich tapestry and we will experience that love which has existed from eternity.

Focus Questions

1. How does the Father reveal the love of the Son and the Spirit?

2. How does the Son reveal the love of the Father and the Spirit?

3. How does the Spirit reveal the love of the Father and the Son?

Holding Steady Together

Now this I say lest anyone should deceive you with persuasive words. For though I am absent in the flesh, yet I am with you in spirit, rejoicing to see your good order and the steadfastness of your faith in Christ. (Colossians 2:4-5)

The Greek word for "deceive" here is *paralogizomai*, which means to miscalculate, reason falsely or mislead. "Beguile" is how the King James Version puts it. The word for "persuasive words" is *pithanologia*, which appears only once in the New Testament. According to *A Greek-English Lexicon of the New Testament*, by Bauer, Arndt and Gingrich, it speaks of the "art of persuasion" and is used here of "*plausible* (but false) *arguments.*"

False teachers can be very charming, feeding you and deceiving you with arguments that sound good on first hearing but fall apart on closer inspection. That is why Paul wants the Jesus believers at Colosse to be woven together in love and have the confidence that comes from knowing and experiencing God in an intimate way through Jesus the Messiah.

Most of these believers Paul has probably never seen in person but he knows about them through Epaphras, who has related to him their faith in Jesus and their love for all believers everywhere. So, though he is not with them "in the flesh," Paul is able to identify with them "in spirit" and understand their spiritual condition. And what he sees in them fills him with joy. He rejoices to see their "good order" and the "steadfastness" of their faith in the Messiah.

The Greek word for "good order" is a military term, which Paul uses metaphorically. It means that they hold the line without any breaches. The word for "steadfastness" is similar. They have been holding steady in their faith against the attacks of the enemy, maintaining a solid formation like a Roman phalanx (a formation of infantry with interlocking shields).

It is important to remember that a line is not a line of one nor can one man form a phalanx all by himself. Paul is not writing to a collection of individuals but to a community of faith. They are not each one left to fend for themselves but are all in this together. They are a tight band of believers with a common love for one another and a common faith in, and love for, the Lord Jesus. There is great strength in that. And so Paul rejoices.

Focus Questions

1. What will protect us from being beguiled by persuasive but false words?

2. What does it mean to be with a person "in spirit?"

3. What is the value of a close military formation?

Walking It Out

As you therefore have received Christ Jesus the Lord, so walk in Him. (Colossians 2:6)

The Jesus believers at Colosse are holding steady together. Paul encourages them now to continue in the path on which they have begun. They "received" Jesus the Messiah. The Greek word, *paralambano*, indicates that Jesus, that is, the message about Him, had been presented to them and that they "took hold" of Him by faith. They learned the "good news" about the Messiah, from Epaphras, who learned it from Paul.

Now they are to "walk" in it, or more accurately, in *Him*, Jesus. "Walk" is a metaphor for how one lives. It is a continuous process, one step after another in a consistent manner. It is progressive, not regressive. That is, it is moving forward, not turning back or straying from the path. It is active, not passive. That is, it is something we do, not something that happens to us. When we receive Jesus, we are *in* Him. That part is passive, part of who we are. But then, being in Him, we proceed in accordance with who He is and who we are in Him. We walk it out.

This particular construction, "Christ Jesus the Lord," notes A. T. Robertson, in *Word Pictures in the New Testament*, is not used anywhere else by Paul. "Hence it is plain that Paul here meets the two forms of Gnostic heresy about the Person of Christ (the recognition of the historical Jesus in his actual humanity against the Docetic Gnostics, the identity of the Christ or Messiah with this historical Jesus against the Cerinthian Gnostics, and the acknowledgment of him as Lord)."

Docetism (from the Greek word *dokeo*, "to seem") taught that Jesus was purely spirit and that his body merely "seemed" to be real. Cerinthianism (after a man named Cerinthus) made a distinction between Jesus and Christ, teaching that Jesus was merely human but that the Christ descended upon him at his baptism. Paul however, in calling Him "Christ Jesus the Lord," emphasizes that the Messiah is human as well as divine.

It is in the fullness of this Jesus, who is Man, Messiah and Lord, that we now live. Having received Him by faith, we continue in the truth of who He really is. Hold steady to that and do not allow yourself to be charmed away from Him.

Focus Questions

1. Why is it important that we keep going forward in our walk with the Lord?

2. Why is it important that Jesus' body was really real?

3. Why is it important that Jesus was not merely a human upon whom the Christ Sprit descended?

Rooted and Built Up in Jesus

As you therefore have received Christ Jesus the Lord, so walk in Him, rooted and built up in Him and established in the faith, as you have been taught, abounding in it with thanksgiving. (Colossians 2:6-7)

Paul wants the Jesus believers as Colosse to continue living according to who Jesus is: both Messiah and Lord. They have begun in that faith and now he wants them to "walk it out."

Verse 7 elaborates. Paul speaks of being "rooted and built up." Mixing these metaphors is not new for Paul, and that should probably tell us something about how important they are for our understanding. In Ephesians 3:17, he speaks of believers being "rooted and grounded in love." In 1 Corinthians 3:9, he says, "For we are God's fellow workers; you are God's field, you are God's building."

"Rooted" is an agricultural metaphor, "built up" is an architectural one. Craig Keener, in *The IVP Bible Background Commentary*, says of this verse, "The Old Testament prophets used this language for Israel (if they obeyed God, they would take root, be planted, built up, etc.), and early Christians probably took this language from their preaching of the Old Testament." Use of this kind of language identifies the New Testament Church along with obedient Old Testament Israel as the people of God.

We should pay attention to the tenses of these words, though they are not readily apparent in most English translations. Kenneth Wuest's *New Testament: An Expanded Translation*, however, captures them well: "having been rooted with the result that your are firmly established, and constantly being built up in Him and constantly being established with reference to the Faith."

In the Greek text, the word for "rooted" is a perfect, passive participle. The *perfect* tense means that it is something that has already been done, with results that continue. The *passive* voice means that it is something that has happened *to* us. God is the one who roots us in Jesus.

The Old Testament often spoke of the people of the Lord as being "planted." For example, those who delight in His instruction are like trees "planted by rivers of water, that brings forth fruit in its season" (Psalm 1:3). In another psalm, the writer sings about God's relationship with Israel, "You have brought a vine out of Egypt; You have cast out the nations, and planted it" (Psalm 80:8-9). The prophet Isaiah speaks of Messiah, who will come to comfort all those who mourn in Zion, "that they may be called trees of righteousness, the planting of the Lord, that He may be glorified" (Isaiah 61:3). This speaks of the work of God in our lives.

In Colossians 2:7, the word for "built up" is a present, passive participle. The *present* tense, in Greek, speaks of a continuing process. Paul shifts metaphors with "built up," which gives us a picture of construction. We are God's building, "having been built on the foundation of the apostles and prophets, Jesus Christ Himself being the chief cornerstone" (Ephesians 2:20). But we are a particular kind of building: "in whom the whole building, being fitted together, grows into a holy temple in the Lord, in whom you also are being built together for a dwelling place of God in the Spirit" (Ephesians 2:21-22). We are God's temple, being built together to be a dwelling place for Him. Peter picks up the same theme, teaching us that we, "as living stones, are being built up a spiritual house," with Jesus as the chief cornerstone (1 Peter 2:-6). Again, this is the work of God in our lives.

The word for "established," *bebaioo*, is also a present, passive participle, indicating a continuing process. It is a word about firmness and stability, and it is used here of being stabilized in the faith. Not just "in faith" but "in *the* faith." The *content* of faith is as important as the *act* of believing it, and the content Paul has in mind is Jesus the Messiah. The *New International Version* translates *bebaioo* as "strengthened." In stability there is strength. As we continue to "walk" in Jesus, we will become stronger in the faith, being strengthened by God. We will not be confused or wavering in faith, or susceptible to those who would try to charm us away from Jesus.

"As you have been taught." It was God who rooted and established them, but He did it through the ministry of Paul and Epaphras. The faith they taught stands in sharp contrast to the message being brought by the gnostic teachers and Jewish mystics who worshiped angels instead of Messiah.

Paul adds a thought about thanksgiving: "abounding in it [the faith] with thanksgiving." Thanksgiving is about being appreciative for what one has received: in this case, the good news of Jesus the Messiah. Thanksgiving is important to the stability and strength of our faith, for what we do not appreciate we will eventually become discontent with and let go.

Focus Questions

1. What is the planting God has done in your life, the foundation He has laid?

2. What is the growth He is bringing into your life, the building He is doing?

3. How does thanksgiving protect us from being "charmed away" from faith in the Lord Jesus?

Don't Be Plundered

Beware lest anyone cheat you through philosophy and empty deceit, according to the tradition of men, according to the basic principles of the world, and not according to Christ. (Colossians 2:8)

"Beware." The Greek word behind it literally means to "see," but Paul uses it here to warn the Jesus believers at Colosse: "Be careful that nobody spoils your faith through intellectualism or high-sounding nonsense" (J. B. Phillips, *The New Testament in Modern English*). "Watch out for people who try to dazzle you with big words and intellectual double-talk. They want to drag you off into endless arguments that never amount to anything" (*The Message*). There are people who would "cheat" you—literally, the word would mean to take you captive and carry you away as spoil—to plunder you! Paul wants believers to be watchful so that we are not robbed of our faith.

Paul does not mean that *all* philosophy is "vain deceit" but he has a particular one in mind. The Greek word *philosophia* literally means "love of wisdom" (*philo*, love and *sophia*, wisdom). The false teachers Paul warns about presented themselves as possessing a special, secret wisdom not available to everyone. They learned to speak persuasively but their philosophy was hollow and deceptive, a toxic mixture of Jewish and pagan folk religion, mystical tradition and occultic teaching that was very strong in the region of Colosse and Laodicea.

"Tradition of men" and "basic principles of the world" (*stoicheion*) is how Paul calls it. The "basic principles" are elemental spirits of nature, the worship or invocation of which is what these false teachers were promoting (as we will see later). *The Message* puts it this way: "They spread their ideas through the empty traditions of human beings and the empty superstitions of spirit beings."

Paul chided the believers at Galatia over the same sort of issue: "But now after you have known God, or rather are known by God, how is it that you turn again to the weak and beggarly elements [*stoicheion*], to which you desire again to be in bondage?" (Galatians 4:9). These were pagan ways of thinking, dressed in Jewish garb and presented as Christian faith. But they were seriously out of alignment with who Jesus is and what He came to do. And they could lead the unwary back into bondage.

That is how such false teachers would plunder us, by pulling us away from Jesus. They cannot pull Him away from us, because He will never deny His own. But they can waste our lives away—our life with Him—by "high-sounding nonsense" and "endless arguments that never amount to anything."

Be very watchful, then, and don't let yourself be plundered and pulled away from Jesus as the center of your faith and life.

Focus Questions

1. Are all philosophies and traditions dangerous?

2. How can we test them?

3. What are some empty philosophies, traditions and superstitions that can draw us away from our focus on the Lord Jesus?

His Fullness and Ours

For in Him dwells all the fullness of the Godhead bodily; and you are complete in Him, who is the head of all principality and power. (Colossians 2:9-10)

There are two mysteries Paul is speaking of here and the second is dependent upon the first: In Jesus the Messiah all the fullness of the Godhead dwells in bodily form. And in Him, Jesus, we ourselves have been made full. Paul's concern is that we be not robbed—plundered!—of these twin truths. For it is in these, not in Jewish ethnos and ritual, or pagan mysticism, that we discover all fullness. It is "fullness" (Greek, *pleroma*) that the false teachers were offering, through ascetic practices and the worship of angels, but were not able to deliver.

All the fullness of God dwells in bodily form. This goes back to Colossians 1:19, where Paul identifies it as a matter of God's sovereign pleasure that all the divine fullness should dwell in Jesus. Now he tweaks that to emphasize that this fullness dwells bodily, in human form. John says the same thing, though a bit differently: "In the beginning was the Word, and the Word was with God, and the Word was God ... and the Word became flesh and dwelt among us" (John 1:1, 14). The nature of this fullness is such that Jesus declared, "He who has seen Me has seen the Father ... Believe Me that I am in the Father and the Father in Me" (John 14:9, 11).

Everything God is can be found in Jesus. Indeed, everything God is, Jesus is. All the fullness of divinity as well as all the fullness of humanity are in Him. He is not half and half, half human and half divine; He is fully both, fully human and fully divine. He is not the demigod the false teachers might have supposed Him to be. He is the God-man, full and complete!

Jesus is filled with all the fullness of God, and those who belong to Jesus are filled with Him. Earlier, Paul revealed the mystery, "Christ in you, the hope of glory" (Colossians 1:29). Jesus is in the Father, and we are in Jesus, and being in Jesus, we are "complete." The Greek word (*pleroo*, from which comes *pleroma*) means to be full or fulfilled and is set in the perfect tense and the passive voice. The perfect tense refers to something that has already been done, with results that continue. The passive voice means that it has been done to or for us, not something we have done to or for ourselves. So, in Jesus we have been made full, with the result that we are now—already!—full and complete in Him. Here is how Peter speaks of this divine completeness:

> *His divine power has given to us all things that pertain to life and godliness, through the knowledge of Him who called us by glory and virtue, by which have been given to us exceedingly great and precious promises, that through these you may be partakers of the divine nature. (2 Peter 1:3-4)*

What the false teachers offered, through the tradition of men and the elemental spirits, but could not deliver, has already been done for us in Jesus the Messiah. And now Paul adds a stinger: This same Jesus is the head over all principality and power. This goes back to Colossians 1:16, where Paul teaches that Jesus is the creator of all things "visible and invisible, whether thrones or dominions or principalities or powers." All of them, including whatever angels and spirits there may be, have been created through Him and for Him. He is Lord over them all, and He is in us and we are in Him.

Focus Questions

1. How is it possible for all the fullness of God to dwell in the bodily form of the Lord Jesus?

2. How is it possible that we have been already been made full and complete in the Lord Jesus?

3. How do we live out these twin truths?

Circumcision of the Heart

In Him you were also circumcised with the circumcision made without hands, by putting off the body of the sins of the flesh, by the circumcision of Christ. (Colossians 2:11)

Here we see one of the issues of the Judaizing influence that was trying to make its way into the Church at Colosse: the matter of circumcision (removal of the foreskin). In the Old Testament, circumcision was a token of the covenant God made with Abraham (Genesis 17:11-14) and was passed down to his descendants as a sign. Every male Israelite was to be circumcised. It marked them out as belonging to the chosen people of God.

Now there were Jewish teachers coming into the churches, saying that Gentiles who believed in Jesus, the Jewish Messiah, needed to be circumcised, and this would make them full and complete members of the people of God. That is contrary to the heart of the gospel, which is that we are made complete in Jesus the Messiah, who is ruler over every principality and power, and in whom all the fullness of God dwells in bodily form (Colossians 2:10).

And yet there is still a circumcision for all those who are in Jesus. As important a sign as physical circumcision was in the Old Testament, and one commanded by God, God was much more concerned with what was going on in the heart. Circumcision was meant to be the outward sign of an inward reality. This was made clear even in the Old Testament.

Therefore circumcise the foreskin of your heart, and be stiff-necked no longer. (Deuteronomy 10:16)

And the LORD your God will circumcise your heart and the heart of your descendants, to love the LORD your God with all your heart and with all your soul, that you may live. (Deuteronomy 30:6)

Circumcise yourselves to the LORD, and take away the foreskins of your hearts. (Jeremiah 4:4)

The physical rite was the cutting away of the flesh and symbolized faithfulness to the covenant God made with Israel. Removing that little fold of skin, however, could not produce what it signified. But Jesus has accomplished for us what physical circumcision never could. Paul says, "In Him you were circumcised." The Greek text has it in the aorist tense and passive voice. The aorist tense means that it has been completed; the passive voice means that it was something done for us, not something we did for ourselves.

This circumcision is one "made without hands." Not a physical one performed by a man with a knife, but a circumcision of the heart. "Putting off the body of the flesh," is how Paul has it here (in the oldest Greek manuscripts). He is not talking about the physical human body but of our sinfulness as a whole. The *New International Version* has it this way: "the putting off of the sinful nature." Paul frequently used the word "flesh" (Greek, *sarx*) to refer to human sinfulness, the state of those without the life and power of God at work in them. The circumcision that Jesus performs, the circumcision of the heart, frees us from the deadness of our fallen human nature and breathes new life, divine life, the life of the Spirit of God, into us.

In his letter to the believers at Rome, Paul speaks of this same reality but in different words and using baptism, which is the outward sign of the inward reality God has accomplished in us through Jesus the Messiah.

> *Therefore we were buried with Him through baptism into death, that just as Christ was raised from the dead by the glory of the Father, even so we also should walk in newness of life. For if we have been united together in the likeness of His death, certainly we also shall be in the likeness of His resurrection, knowing this, that our old man was crucified with Him, that the body of sin might be done away with, that we should no longer be slaves of sin. For he who has died has been freed from sin. (Romans 6:4-7)*

In the Old Testament, circumcision was a sign of who God's chosen people were, through whom He would bring the redemption of the whole world. Now what matters is not circumcision or uncircumcision, but "faith working through love" (Galatians 5:6). What Paul is talking about is faith in Jesus, and His love working in and through us.

Focus Questions

1. What is the new reality God has accomplished in us through the Lord Jesus?

2. In this new reality, how does faith work through love?

3. What is your understanding about baptism?

Buried with Him, Raised with Him

Buried with Him in baptism, in which you also were raised with Him through faith in the working of God, who raised Him from the dead. (Colossians 2:12)

Paul quickly moves from one sign to another, from circumcision to baptism. In verse 11, he contrasted physical circumcision with a non-physical one, a circumcision of the heart. This circumcision is one Jesus does for us and is "made without hands." It is the "putting off the body of the sins of the flesh." That is, it frees us from the sinfulness of human nature, which is put off, stripped from us like old clothes, because it is dead and does not have the life that comes from God.

All that is left for a body that is dead is to be buried. Which brings us to verse 12, where Paul explains to the believers at Colosse that they were buried together with Him in baptism. Baptism was practiced in the Old Testament as "various washings" (Hebrews 9:10), rituals of purification. But in the New Testament it is given new meaning for the community of Jesus believers. It signifies the spiritual circumcision that Jesus has performed for us. It says that we are dead to sin and that we have been buried together with Jesus, as if in the tomb. But that is not all, for we have also been raised with Him.

Pay close attention to tense, voice and mood in this verse: "Buried with Him" and "raised with Him" are in the Greek aorist tense, indicating completed action. Both are in the passive voice, indicating what was done to and for us, not something we did for ourselves. However, the moods are different. "Buried" is a participle—"having been buried," as the *Lexham English Bible* has it—and "raised" is in the indicative mood. The two go together: Being raised with the Lord Jesus completes the action begun with having been buried with Him.

Just as Jesus was buried but did not remain in the grave because God raised Him up, so baptism shows that that we, too, have been "buried together with Him" and also "raised together with Him." Baptism is a physical sign indicating a spiritual reality, but there is also a physical resurrection coming, of which the resurrection of Jesus' physical body from the dead is the beginning (Paul details this in 1 Corinthians 15). So baptism also prophesies our future bodily resurrection even as it portrays Jesus' bodily resurrection.

However, we have already been raised spiritually with Jesus. How was this done? The *NKJV* says it was "through faith in the working of God," as do many other versions. So it is usually taken to mean that God raised us up through our faith in the working of God, or that we appropriate this truth through our faith. Indeed, we do come to God by faith. "By grace you have been saved through faith," Paul says (Ephesians 2:8). However, although the Greek text can be translated as "through faith *in* the working of God" it can also be "through the faith *of* the working of God."

So there is another way of approaching this. Actually, there are a few different ways. One is to take it as Weymouth translates it, "through faith produced within you by God" (*The New Testament in Modern Speech*). Adam Clarke's commentary also treats it this way, as faith produced by the working, or energy (the Greek word for "working" is *energeo*) of God. This would go along with what Paul teaches elsewhere, that faith is the gift of God (Ephesians 2:8) and comes by hearing the Word of God (Romans 10:17).

Yet there is still another way to translate this phrase, and the one I am most inclined to. The Greek word for "faith," *pistis*, can also mean "faithfulness," and I think this is one place where that fits better. The emphasis here is not on us but on Jesus, in whom all the fullness of God dwells in bodily form (Colossians 2:9), and what He is doing in us. It seems to me, then, that what Paul has in mind here is not so much about *our faith*, even though that faith comes to us from God, as it is about *God's faithfulness*.

Having been buried together with Jesus, we have also been raised up together with Him through the faithfulness of God's work. Baptism is an outward, visible sign of this inward, invisible reality.

Focus Questions

1. How does baptism help you think about our death with the Lord Jesus?

2. How does baptism help you think about our resurrection and new life with the Lord Jesus?

3. Which do you think is more important—our faith or God's faithfulness?

Side Slips Forgiven

And you, being dead in your trespasses and the uncircumcision of your flesh, He has made alive together with Him, having forgiven you all trespasses. (Colossians 2:13)

Paul continues here about baptism and the reality it signifies. We were dead, we were buried, we have been made alive together with the Lord Jesus, and God has forgiven us of all trespasses.

The Greek word for "trespasses," *paraptoma* is an interesting one. *Strong's Greek Dictionary* calls it a "side slip," which puts me in mind of Paul Simon's old song, "Slip Sliding Away." *Vine's Expository Dictionary* calls it "a false step, a blunder." The *Bauer-Arndt-Gingrich Greek Lexicon* calls it a "false step." Our English word "trespass" comes from a compound Latin word that literally means to "pass across." When we trespass, we have passed across a line we should not have crossed.

In the Bible, "trespass" refers to stepping outside the boundaries of God's law, whether by unintentional error or by willful transgression. The result is death, and it has affected us all, just as we were also all affected by what Paul calls "the uncircumcision of your flesh," which is human nature in rebellion against God and devoid of the life that comes from Him. The good news is that though we were once dead in these things, we have been made alive together with Jesus the Messiah. This is possible because, in Jesus, God has forgiven us all our trespasses.

The Greek word for "forgiven" here, *charizomai*, is not the one we usually find in the New Testament, though Paul does favor it in his letters. The root word is *charis*, "grace" or "favor." *Charizomai* speaks of what is given or granted or released because of grace. The root for our English word "forgive" is from the Latin word, *perdonare* ("pardon"), which means to give thoroughly or wholeheartedly. So it is a good translation here. In Jesus, God has graciously pardoned us, released us from all the ways we have violated His commandments.

Focus Questions

1. Think of a time when you were in rebellion against God. Did you feel alive, or dead?

2. Did you feel like you were in bondage, or walking in freedom?

3. Have you experienced what it means to be made alive together with the Lord Jesus?

The Great Wipe Out

Having wiped out the handwriting of requirements that was against us, which was contrary to us. And He has taken it out of the way, having nailed it to the cross. (Colossians 2:14)

Paul tells the Jesus believers at Colosse that God made them alive together with King Jesus the Messiah, "having forgiven you all trespasses," or as the *Unvarnished New Testament* puts it, "freely letting us off for all our transgressions."

But there is more to it. Having forgiven all trespasses, yes, but also, "having wiped out the handwriting of requirements that was against us." The use of the word "handwriting" in this context has a technical meaning, commonly referring to a legal document, a bond, a certificate of indebtedness. The debt we owed was great and the document against us was "hostile to us" (*Lexham English Bible*).

Paul is being metaphorical here, of course, but he does have something in mind with the writ of "requirements." The Greek word is *dogma* and in the New Testament was used of decrees and ordinances. The *English Standard Version* translates it as "legal demands." The *Good News Bible* calls it "binding rules." What Paul is talking about is the Law of Moses. The Law itself is holy and right and good (Romans 7:12). But for those who violated it—which was everyone—it held condemnation.

But look at what God has done in Jesus the Messiah. He not only wiped out the debt note, He wiped out the ordinance along with it! He cancelled it, erased it, washed it all out. "He obliterated the arrest warrant with our names on it that had been in force against us, with all its dogmas" (*UNT*).

How did He wipe it all out? He nailed it to the cross in the body of Jesus. Jesus took it all off of us and put it on Himself. "Hauled it right out of the way and nailed it to the cross" (*UNT*). Now it no longer stands against us. It no longer has a voice to condemn us. We are now "dead to the Law," Paul says (Romans 7:4), and it is dead to us. "Therefore there is now no condemnation for those who are in Christ Jesus. For the law of the Spirit of life in Christ Jesus has set you free from the law of sin and of death" (Romans 8:1-2).

Focus Questions

1. How does the cross wipe out the legal demands of the Law?

2. If the Law that condemned us has been wiped out, where does the sense of condemnation come from?

3. If we are dead to the Law, how then should we live?

Disarming the Powers

Having disarmed principalities and powers, He made a public spectacle of them, triumphing over them in it. (Colossians 2:15)

In Jesus the Messiah, God has not only forgiven us all the ways we have stepped across the boundaries of the Law, He has also wiped out the debt we owed, the indictment of the Law, which could only condemn and never redeem. Jesus carried it away and nailed it to the cross in His own body. But there is more and it is just as important: At the cross, Jesus disarmed the principalities and powers. It was such entities as these that false teachers were presenting as keys to divine understanding, but which lead only to oppression. Paul's message here is that Jesus has defeated them.

The principalities and powers are not human rulers and leaders, they are spiritual entities *behind* human rulers and leaders and governments, who influence the affairs of humanity in systemic ways. Daniel 10, for instance, speaks of the "prince of Persia" and the "prince of Greece," but these are not human beings, for the angel Gabriel (identified in Daniel 8:16) and Michael the archangel engage directly in battle with them. Jews from the Second Temple era understood such "princes" to be chief angels who had fallen and became a corrupting influence in the world. The conflicts that happen in human history reflect the warfare that takes place in the spiritual realm. In his letter to the Jesus believers at Corinth, Paul speaks of the principalities and powers that put Jesus up on the cross, though he calls them by a different name.

> *However, we speak wisdom among those who are mature, yet not the wisdom of this age, nor of the rulers of this age, who are coming to nothing. But we speak the wisdom of God in a mystery, the hidden wisdom which God ordained before the ages for our glory, which none of the rulers of this age knew; for had they known, they would not have crucified the Lord of glory. (1 Corinthians 2:6-8)*

This reference to the "rulers of this age" runs deeper than Pontius Pilate or Herod or the Jewish leaders who despised Jesus. It digs down to the spiritual entities and demonic forces that influenced and even manipulated them. So the conflict was not merely between Jesus and Pilate or Herod or the Jewish leaders in the physical realm—that was just an outward manifestation—but there was a battle going on in the dimension of the spirit.

The principalities and powers wanted to put a stop to Jesus because He is the Messiah, that is, He is the one "anointed" (which is what "Messiah" means) by God to be King over all the nations. They desperately needed to keep the kingdom of God from being established in the earth because that would signal the end for them. Jesus said, "But if I cast out demons by the Spirit of God, surely the kingdom of God has come upon you" (Matthew 12:28).

The "rulers of this age" knew very well what was at stake for them. Using the "wisdom of this age," they thought they had the answer: Put Jesus on the cross, because a crucified Messiah would be a contradiction in terms. They threw everything they had at Him, a series of humiliations ending in death on the cross. And when Jesus breathed out His last that Friday afternoon, they thought they had won.

But God had a greater wisdom, and it soon became apparent that the principalities and powers had not defeated Jesus at all. Quite the opposite. He had disarmed *them*, stripped them of their power by the power of God. As the apostle John said, "The Son of God appeared for this purpose, to destroy the works of the devil" (1 John 3:8). It was through the cross and the resurrection that these entities were defeated. Paul writes about this in his letter to the believers at Ephesus, praying that they might know

> *the exceeding greatness of His power toward us who believe, according to the working of His mighty power which He worked in Christ when He raised Him from the dead and seated Him at His right hand in the heavenly places, far above all principality and power and might and dominion, and every name that is named, not only in this age but also in that which is to come. (Ephesians 1:19-21).*

Jesus not only disarmed the principalities and powers, He "made a public spectacle of them, triumphing over them." This "public spectacle" was a victory parade, a triumphal procession, such as kings or generals would make after a great conquest. They would lead the defeated foe, plundered and powerless, along with the spoils of war, for all the people to see. The powers have been broken and we have been set free. God's purpose is that "that now the manifold wisdom of God might be made known by the church to the principalities and powers in the heavenly places" (Ephesians 3:10).

So we can say, along with Paul, "Now thanks be to God who always leads us in triumph in Christ, and through us diffuses the fragrance of His knowledge in every place" (2 Corinthians 2:14).

Focus Questions

1. Why is it important that Jesus has disarmed the principalities and powers?

2. How do we walk out this victory that Jesus has won for us?

3. What does this signal about the turmoil of the nations?

Out of the Shadows

So let no one judge you in food or in drink, or regarding a festival or a new moon or sabbaths, which are a shadow of things to come, but the substance is of Christ. (Colossians 2:16-17)

"So"—that is conclusion, the *therefore* that follows from the preceding verses (and some versions do translate it as "therefore"). It reaches back as far as verse 8, "Beware lest anyone cheat you through philosophy and empty deceit, according to the tradition of men, according to the basic principles of the world, and not according to Christ."

Dietary rules and the calendar of festivals were important in the Law of Moses. The dietary laws were one way of setting apart the people of Israel as the people of God. The festivals reminded them of past deliverance and how God had created them as His covenant people, but they also pointed forward to the final deliverance God had for them when He would set the world right through Messiah.

However, these things were all "shadows." Their significance was not in themselves but in what they pointed to—that that which cast those shadows. Once the substance comes, the shadow is no longer the focus. The "substance," the reality to which the shadows point, is Jesus the Messiah, and He has now come, bringing God's redemption into the world. He not only brought forgiveness for all our "side slips," He also wiped out the indictment that accused us—the Law! He took it and nailed it to the cross (v. 14). What is more, He disarmed all the principalities and powers—the demonic entities behind the human rulers and systems that crucified Him—and made a "public spectacle of them, triumphing over them in it" (v. 15).

"Therefore," Paul says, "Let no one judge you." Do not let anyone condemn you or look down on you because of what you do or do not eat or drink, or whether or not you join in the traditional festivals or celebrations. To follow his analogy, do not let anyone drag you away from Jesus the Messiah back into the shadows that were cast by Him and pointed to Him in the first place. That is exactly what the false teachers, with their blend of Jewish folk religion and ideas of the occult, were trying to do. It was a misuse, by the principalities and powers, of the Law of Moses and it brought only condemnation and bondage.

But Jesus the Messiah has delivered us from all that, and our focus, like that of the Law and the prophets of the Old Testament, is to be set firmly on Him.

Focus Questions

1. What are some of the ways human tradition tries to judge us and drag us away from the Lord Jesus?

2. How does Jesus bring the substance or fulfillment to what the shadows pointed toward?

3. What now sets apart and marks believers as the people of God?

Keeping Focus

Let no one cheat you of your reward, taking delight in false hu-
mility and worship of angels, intruding into those things which
he has not seen, vainly puffed up by his fleshly mind, and not
holding fast to the Head, from whom all the body, nourished and
knit together by joints and ligaments, grows with the increase
that is from God. (Colossians 2:18-19)

Imagine this: You have run the race and you have won. You are just about to receive the prize, when a judge comes over, taps you on the shoulder and says, "This does not belong to you—you have been disqualified." That is the kind of picture Paul paints here.

The believers at Colosse had come to faith in Jesus the Messiah. They had been buried with Him in baptism and raised with Him through the faithfulness of God. They were in the "winner's circle." But then certain teachers came with elements of Judaism, folk religion and esoteric philosophies and told them that what they had—the Lord Jesus—was not enough. They told them that they needed to have special hidden knowledge, certain ascetic practices and unusual revelatory experiences if they were going to know the fullness of God. Otherwise they would not be qualified for the reward.

Paul's answer to all that was, if I may paraphrase, "Don't let them rob you of what it means to be the Church, the body of Messiah!" These teachers submitted themselves to angels, through fasting and acts of self-denial, invoking them for protection from demonic powers. They presented themselves as humble but then went about bragging how they were initiated into the "deeper mysteries" and how they saw visions. Their egos were inflated by the kind of thinking that comes from fallen human nature. They were caught up in themselves.

But these are symptoms. The real problem was this: They were not connected to the Head. Imagine a body without a head, still trying to carry on and function—the proverbial "chicken with its head cut off." That is Paul's assessment of these false teachers. They were not connected to the Head of the body. That is, they had no vital relationship with Jesus, who is the head of the Church (Colossians 1:18). They were focused on themselves, their philosophies, their practices, their experiences—but not on Jesus.

Paul's teaching is that *everything* we need is found in Jesus the Messiah. Divine fullness does not come from angels or visions or secret knowledge or self-abasements. We already have all the fullness of God in Him. "For in Him dwells all the fullness of the Godhead bodily, and you are complete in Him" (Colossians 1:9-10). Anything that pulls our focus away from Him robs us of knowing His completeness, and our completeness in Him. He is the head, and it is only in Him that we grow together as His body, with all the life that comes from God.

Focus Questions

1. How can humility become false and a form of pride?

2. What does true humility look like?

3. Why is our relationship to the Lord Jesus important to our relationship with each other?

Live as Free

Therefore, if you died with Christ from the basic principles of the world, why, as though living in the world, do you subject

> *yourselves to regulations—"Do not touch, do not taste, do not handle," which all concern things which perish with the using—according to the commandments and doctrines of men? These things indeed have an appearance of wisdom in self-imposed religion, false humility, and neglect of the body, but are of no value against the indulgence of the flesh. (Colossians 2:20-23)*

By "if," Paul does not question whether the believers at Colosse have died with Messiah—he has already taught them that they have been "buried with Christ in baptism" (Colossians 2:12). But he is challenging them to live according to that truth. What happened to Jesus at the cross is counted by God as having happened to us, in our place and for our benefit. Once we were dead *in* the sinfulness of fallen human nature. Now, having died with Jesus, we are dead *to* it. Our "side slips" have been forgiven, the regulation that condemned us has been wiped out and the principalities have been disarmed.

Since those who are in Jesus are dead to all these things, why should we live as if we were still subject to them? They now have no authority over us. Yet religious teachers were coming around the believers at Colosse and teaching them that they must follow ascetic practices and regulations. Such rules and regulations are not from God but are the "commandments and doctrines of men." Paul could be referring to Isaiah 29:13, where God says,

> *Inasmuch as these people draw near with their mouths*
> *And honor Me with their lips,*
> *But have removed their hearts far from Me,*
> *And their fear toward Me is taught by the commandment of men.*

These things might appear to be wisdom, according to how the world thinks and acts, but it is not the wisdom that comes from God. It is "self-imposed religion." It presents itself as humility, with neglect of the body as a way of overcoming the sinful nature, but it actually has the opposite effect—it ends up indulging the sinful nature through the insidiousness of pride.

The problem is, "Don't eat, don't drink, don't touch" is a focus on things, on regulations, on religion, on ourselves, and not on Jesus the Messiah, who has already overcome the sinful nature and defeated the satanic powers. Our focus and our thinking, then, need to match up with that new reality, then we will learn how to stand in that victory.

Focus Questions

1. What is the difference between being dead *in* sin and dead *to* sin?

2. Why does "self-imposed religion" so often focus on external things, on rules and checklists instead of the heart?

3. Why does the checklist mentality turn out to be so ineffective against the "indulgence of the flesh?"

Living from a Higher Realm

If then you were raised with Christ, seek those things which are above, where Christ is, sitting at the right hand of God. Set your mind on things above, not on things on the earth. (Colossians 3:1-2)

Paul has already settled the issue of whether believers in Jesus the Messiah have been buried and raised with Him. Earlier, he affirmed that we have been "buried with Him in baptism" and likewise "raised with Him" through the faithful work of God (Colossians 2:12). Now Paul is building on the significance of that. So we can take the "if" here as rhetorical.

Since, then, those who believe in Jesus have been raised from the dead with Him, we are now to seek those things which are "above." This is a reference to heaven, of course, but not in the way many people are accustomed to thinking about it—that is, as some place way far away, at the edge of the universe, perhaps, and off into the vagueness of the future. In that sort of view, heaven is mostly a destination and does not have much to do with earth, except that God or one of His angels pops in every now and then to work some little miracle. But that is not at all what Paul has in mind.

No, Paul conceives of heaven as a realm that is very close to us, a realm of which we are already a part. In Ephesians, he speaks of it as "the heavenlies." In the heavenlies, we have already been blessed with every spiritual blessing (Ephesians 1:3). In the heavenlies, we have already been raised up with Jesus the Messiah and seated with Him at the right hand of the Father (Ephesians 2:6). In the heavenlies, we are part of the manifold wisdom of God being made known to the principalities and powers—the same powers that were disarmed by Jesus at the cross (Ephesians 3:10). It is not a *distant* realm but a *higher* one, in both position and priority.

This is now what we are to seek, the things that are of *that* realm. The Greek word for "seek" here is the same one used in Matthew 6:33, where Jesus says, "But *seek* first the kingdom of God and His righteousness." There, Jesus was speaking of the kingdom. Here, Paul is speaking of the King—Jesus. We are to seek those things which are above, where

Jesus the Messiah is enthroned, *seated at the right hand of God*. For Paul, this is enthronement. We can see this in his letter to the Jesus believers at Ephesus, where he speaks about the working of God's mighty power,

> *which He worked in Christ when He raised Him from the dead and seated Him at His right hand in the heavenly places, far above all principality and power and might and dominion, and every name that is named, not only in this age but also in that which is to come. And He put all things under His feet, and gave Him to be head over all things to the church, which is His body, the fullness of Him who fills all in all. (Ephesians 1:19-23)*

To seek the kingdom and the things that are above is not an act of curiosity or idle speculation. We *seek* them in order to *find* them, that we may know and benefit from them.

"Set your mind on things above, not on things on the earth," Paul adds. This is to be our focus now, the lens through which we view everything, the perspective from which we think about and relate to everything. Because we are new creatures who are no longer under the authority of principalities and powers. We no longer have to look at things through the old lens of those broken powers. We can begin to see things as heaven sees them.

Seeking the things above is not about *abandoning* or *escaping* the earth. We seek the things which are above for the *sake* of the earth. Jesus taught us to pray for the kingdom of God to come and the will of God to be done *on earth as it is in heaven*. We are now to look at everything from the perspective of that higher realm so that it may become a reality on earth. Heaven is not our final destination, earth is. We have been raised with Jesus in the spiritual realm but one day we will receive the resurrection of our physical bodies as well, just as

Jesus' own physical body was raised from the dead, and we shall dwell upon the earth. For heaven and earth will become one.

Heaven is not our final *destination*, it is our *source*. Right here, right now. We come *from* heaven, we live *from* heaven. We live on the earth but with the life of heaven at work in us. That is why we are to seek the things that are of that realm, to set our thinking on how heaven operates. Because it corresponds with who we really are in Jesus and who He is in us. Should we not view things from the perspective of where we are now seated with Him? Then we will be able to manifest the reality of heaven on earth.

Focus Questions

1. What is your conception of the realm of heaven?

2. What is your conception of the relationship between heaven and earth?

3. In what ways might the reality of heaven be made manifest on earth, that is, the will of God being done on earth as it is in heaven?

Hidden in God

For you died, and your life is hidden with Christ in God. When Christ who is our life appears, then you also will appear with Him in glory. (Colossians 3:3-4)

All who believe in the Lord Jesus have a new life now, one that is from a higher realm. Not the old realm to which we had once become accustomed, one influenced and controlled by principalities and powers. These have been disarmed now and we are no longer subject to them. We died to them. Oh, they are still present in the world and they still have a voice, but they no longer have any authority over us. The only power they hold now is the power we yield or attribute to them. Jesus has been given all authority in heaven and on earth (Matthew 28:18). His authority extends over all the powers and they must all bow and acknowledge that He is Lord (Philippians 2:9-11).

Jesus the Messiah is now the source of our lives. Indeed, He *is* our life. In his letter to the Jesus believers of Galatia, Paul made this declaration: "I have been crucified with Christ; it is no longer I who live, but Christ lives in me; and the life which I now live in the flesh I live by faith in the Son of God, who loved me and gave Himself for me" (Galatians 2:20). The life of the Messiah is now at work in us—He lives in us, we live in Him.

But this new life is "hidden." The Greek word is *crypto*, which is, of course, where we get our English word "cryptic." This life is not apparent to the senses. It is not perceptible to the ordinary ways we were once accustomed to seeing things when we were trapped under the influences of the principalities and powers. However, it is not hidden in those powers or in the hierarchy of angels, as the gnostic teachers might have imagined. No, our life is now hidden with the Messiah, hidden in God.

Once, when we were spiritually dead, we were disconnected from the life of God. We could not perceive or understand that life. But now, in Jesus the Messiah, we are dead to everything alien to that life—those things no longer have any power over us and we no longer have to yield to them. Because we are now made alive to God. As Paul said to the believers at Rome, "Likewise you also, reckon yourselves to be dead indeed to sin, but alive to God in Christ Jesus our Lord" (Romans 6:11).

When the Messiah "appears," that is, when He comes again, this life we have in Him will be revealed in all its glory—the glory of Jesus Himself. This glory is not a place, as some Christians tend to think, but an expression of identity. It is a revelation, the unveiling of who we are in Jesus and who He is in us. The apostle John says it this way:

> *Beloved, now we are children of God; and it has not yet been revealed what we shall be, but we know that when He is revealed, we shall be like Him, for we shall see Him as He is. And everyone who has this hope in Him purifies himself, just as He is pure. (1 John 3:2-3)*

John concludes from this that everyone who has this "hope" purifies himself, just as Jesus is pure. In other words, because we have the expectation that who we are in Jesus and who He is in us will one day be revealed in all its glory, we no longer have to live according to what we once were. We are free to begin living this new life we have in Him and become who we really are.

Focus Questions

1. In what way have we died? In what way have we been made alive?

2. How does this new life we have in Jesus turn human systems upside down?

3. How might this new life be revealed in us even now?

Putting Old Ways to Death

Therefore put to death your members which are on the earth: fornication, uncleanness, passion, evil desire, and covetousness, which is idolatry. Because of these things the wrath of God is coming upon the sons of disobedience, in which you yourselves once walked when you lived in them. (Colossians 3:5-7)

All our "side slips" (trespasses) have been forgiven. The indictment that accused and condemned us has been nailed to the cross in the body of Jesus. The principalities and powers have been disarmed. We are dead to all these things. But that is not a license to go back to the old ways of the world and the sinful behaviors that once held us in bondage.

Paul gives a brief list of sins that are mostly sexual in nature and were apparently prevalent in the culture of that day as well as in the false teaching that was being hawked.

- ❧ The Greek word for "fornication" is *porneia* (from which we get the word "pornography") and refers to any illicit sexual intercourse.
- ❧ "Uncleanness" speaks of sexual immorality and the pursuit of such.
- ❧ "Passion" is lust or inordinate affection.
- ❧ "Evil desire" is licentiousness.
- ❧ "Covetousness," or some versions say "greed," is insatiable hunger or desire.
- ❧ "Idolatry" is giving priority to anything other than God.

This list sounds very much like modern Western culture with its insatiable desire for all kinds of sexual behaviors and abuses to the point that sex has become a very prominent idol. They are part of the old ways of a fallen world and God's wrath will come on all of them. Such perversions and idolatries may have been part of who we once were but they have no place in our new life in Jesus.

Some strains of the false teaching Paul has been addressing believed that matter is inherently evil and the physical body beyond redemption. Therefore, they reasoned, it does not matter what one does in or with the body. But Paul will have none of that. The body is not beyond redemption, it will be transformed in the resurrection to come, when Jesus returns. For He is the "firstborn from the dead" (Colossians 1:18) and the guarantee of our own bodily resurrection (1 Corinthians 15). So, *yes!* It *does* matter what we do with our bodies. We now have new life in Jesus the Messiah, as well as the promise of the resurrection of the body, and how we live now should demonstrate that reality.

Paul says, then, "Put to death your members which are on the earth." These "members" are the appendages, the remnants of the way we used to live in the world before we received this new life in the Lord Jesus. We are now dead to them. Though they still have a voice, it is an echo that no longer has any authority, and the only power it has over us is whatever power we yield to it. "Put to death" means to make it dead, deprive it of its power, destroy its strength.

How do we do that? Not by beating ourselves up, treating our bodies harshly or trying to keep a list of rules and regulations. As we saw earlier, such things "are of no value against the indulgence of the flesh" (Colossians 2:23). But Paul has already given us the answer: We are already dead to these things! We died to them with Jesus the Messiah. We have also been raised with Him and He is now our life. What is needed now is to live in the truth of that. In other words, it is a matter of faith—that is, believing the truth of who Jesus is in us and who we are in Him. In his letter to the believers at Rome, Paul put it this way:

Likewise you also, reckon yourselves to be dead indeed to sin, but alive to God in Christ Jesus our Lord. Therefore do not let sin reign in your mortal body, that you should obey it in its lusts. And do not present your members as instruments of unrighteousness to sin, but present yourselves to God as being alive from the dead, and your members as instruments of righteousness to God. For sin shall not have dominion over you, for you are not under law but under grace. (Romans 6:11-14)

To "reckon" means to account it to be so, to treat it as the truth that we are indeed dead to sin and alive to God. When temptation comes and the voice of the old ways tries to reassert itself, we do not have to let it have any place in us. It has been stripped of its power and we do not have to give any of it back. Instead, we answer with the truth: We are now dead to sin and alive to God (it helps to make this a personal declaration: "*I* am now dead to sin and alive to God"). Instead of yielding ourselves to the old, fading echoes of who we once were, we present ourselves to God, yielding ourselves to Him. The grace of God and the power of the new life we have in Jesus accomplishes in us what rules and regulations never could.

Focus Questions

1. Why does it matter what we do with our bodies now?

2. How do we "put to death" the remnants and silence the old voices?

3. How does asserting the truth of who we are in Jesus help us?

A Renewed Image

But now you yourselves are to put off all these: anger, wrath, malice, blasphemy, filthy language out of your mouth. Do not lie to one another, since you have put off the old man with his deeds, and have put on the new man who is renewed in knowledge according to the image of Him who created him, where there is neither Greek nor Jew, circumcised nor uncircumcised, barbarian, Scythian, slave nor free, but Christ is all and in all. (Colossians 3:8-11)

In the previous section, the sins Paul listed were mostly of a sexual nature. It should be obvious that these do not come from the new life we have in Jesus but are alien to it. They are part of the old life and come under the judgment of God. But now Paul brings another list of things to "put off." This list is mostly about our attitudes toward one another, how we treat each other. It largely concerns our communication, that is, our mouths and how we speak to one another.

The things in this second list might not seem as wrong to us at the things in the first. But for Paul, the things in this list are just as bad, if not worse. For one thing, they are not as obvious and, consequently, are the kind of things that Jesus believers are more likely to get caught up in. We pretty well know we should avoid the obvious sins, but the less obvious ones can slip in easily "under the radar." However, they are just as destructive to our lives and just as harmful to our relationships with one another.

∾ *Anger and wrath.* The Greek words for these are very similar in meaning. "Anger" appears to be a disposition, and "wrath" the expression of that disposition.
∾ *Malice.* Ill-will toward others.

~ *Blasphemy.* Slander, speaking ill of others, whether about God or other people.

~ *Filthy or obscene language.* Weymouth translates this as "foul-mouthed abuse" (*New Testament in Modern Speech*).

Paul adds one more category of communication and sets it out by itself: "Do not lie to one another." There is no room for deceitfulness with each other. The reason he gives here is this: "You have put off the old man with his deeds, and have put on the new man."

"Put off" and "put on." It is like a man changing out of filthy rags into a fine, new suit. He puts off all the old clothes and is made clean. Afterwards, he does not put those old rags back on; they are fit only for the trash bin. Instead, he puts on the new clothes, the fine suit. That is what Paul pictures for us here. We have been washed clean in Jesus and made new with His life. The old way of life no longer fits. It does not reflect who we now are in Jesus and it stinks of death. We have already put off the "old man" and put on the new—it happened when we received King Jesus as our own. Having put on the new man, why should we go back and wear any of the raggedy, stinking clothes of the old man.

This new life we have put on, the new person we have become in Jesus, is "renewed in knowledge according to the image of Him who created him." From the beginning of creation, God made man to be in His image, to be like Him (Genesis 1:26). When Adam rebelled against God, this image was marred in the fall, but in Jesus it has been made new. Now our thinking is being renewed, made new by knowing God through Jesus the Messiah.

In his letter to the believers at Rome, Paul speaks in a similar way about the renewal of the mind: "Do not be conformed to this world, but be transformed by the renewing of your mind, that you may prove what is that good and acceptable and perfect will of God"

(Romans 12:1-2). To be conformed to the world, the way it thinks and behaves, would not reflect who we really are in Jesus. We need to be *transformed*, so that our outward being reveals the true nature of our inward being and the new life we have. We are transformed by the renewing of our minds, to think God's thoughts after Him, walk in His ways and fulfill the destiny He has for us.

God's purpose, Paul tells us, is to conform us to the "image of His Son" (Romans 8:29). Jesus is the perfect image of God, and as we are conformed to Him, we are being conformed to the original image in which God created humanity, so that we may be fruitful and multiply, to fill the earth and have dominion (Genesis 1:28). In this way, the will of God is done on earth as it is in heaven.

In this new life we have in Jesus, and the new creation of which we are now a part, it does not matter if one is a Jew or a Gentile. Those categories are no longer operative, the distinction between circumcision and uncircumcision no longer holds, the uncultured and the uncouth are both welcomed, and the slave is on equal footing with the free. All that matters is King Jesus the Messiah, who we are in Him and who He is in us.

Focus Questions

1. Why must we put off these old ways of dealing with one another? What harm do they do?

2. Why is there so often a difference between the new person we really are in Jesus and the way we act?

3. Paul speaks often in his letters about the *image* of God. Why is this *image* so important?

Clothes for Your New Life

Therefore, as the elect of God, holy and beloved, put on tender mercies, kindness, humility, meekness, longsuffering; bearing with one another, and forgiving one another, if anyone has a complaint against another; even as Christ forgave you, so you also must do. But above all these things put on love, which is the bond of perfection. (Colossians 3:12-14)

Paul has shown us that the clothes of our old identity do not belong to the new identity of who we now are in Jesus the Messiah. They must be *put off*. But he does not leave us with nothing to wear. Now he speaks of what we are to *put on*, things that reflect our new life in Jesus. But first, he briefly reminds us of that identity: We are "the elect of God, holy and beloved." Chosen of God. Set apart by God. Dearly loved by God.

Our identity as the elect of God is in Jesus the Messiah. *He* is the one God has chosen, the one He has anointed, the one He has established to have dominion over the earth. Jesus is the one of whom the Father said, "This is My beloved Son, in whom I am well pleased" (Matthew 3:17). Remember that Paul writes to the believers here as "saints and faithful brethren *in Christ*." It is in Jesus the Messiah, the Elect One, that we ourselves are chosen, set apart and dearly loved by God. We are "accepted in the Beloved," that is, in Jesus (Ephesians 1:6). Not only individually, but all of us together in Him.

These, then, are the kind of clothes we have now for our new life in the Beloved. Notice that, like the list of things we are to put off, these are all about our relationships and how we treat one another. Paul speaks over two dozen times in his letters about the ways we should treat each other, and several times about the ways we should not. (You can find these by searching Paul's letters for "one" plus "another.")

- *Tender mercies.* Not merely acts of mercy but an attitude of tenderhearted affection and compassion.
- *Kindness.* Gentleness and goodness toward each other.
- *Humility.* Not lifting ourselves up and looking down on each other.
- *Longsuffering.* Being patient with each other.
- *Bearing with one another.* Being tolerant toward each other, putting up with each other even when it is difficult (as indeed it sometimes can be).
- *Forgiving one another.* Paul expands on this one, which should tell us something about how important it is. If we have a quarrel with or complaint against anyone, we are to forgive, just as Jesus has forgiven us.

All of these are expressions of love. Love bundles them all together. Jesus said that all the law and the prophets are fulfilled in the command to love God with everything in us and love our neighbor as ourselves (Matthew 22:37-40). Jesus is the perfect fulfillment of that. The early gnostic teachers located perfection or completeness in understanding the mysteries, the secret wisdom they brought. But Paul identifies love, the kind that comes from God, the kind that Jesus demonstrated, as the bond of perfection. As we set our hearts to love each other with that kind of self-giving love, we are brought together into completeness and maturity, well-suited to the destiny God has for us.

Focus Questions

1. Why does Paul spend so much time, here and elsewhere, on how believers should treat each other?

2.   Why does forgiveness receive such prominence in this list?

3.   How do all these things tell us about love?

The Word That Qualifies Us

And let the peace of God rule in your hearts, to which also you were called in one body; and be thankful. Let the word of Christ dwell in you richly in all wisdom, teaching and admonishing one another in psalms and hymns and spiritual songs, singing with grace in your hearts to the Lord. And whatever you do in word or deed, do all in the name of the Lord Jesus, giving thanks to God the Father through Him. (Colossians 3:15-17)

Paul continues his talk on what the new life we have in Jesus should look like on us, with everything bound together with love as the mature and complete expression of that life. Now he shifts the analogy. "Let the peace of God rule in your hearts." The Greek word for "rule" is *brabeuo*, which speaks of a judge in an athletic competition. We came across it earlier, in Colossians 2:18, where Paul said, "Let no one *cheat* you of your reward." There the form was *katabrabeuo*, to "judge against," and Paul was talking about the false teachers who were trying to disqualify believers by teaching them they needed something besides King Jesus. But here, it is the peace of God that comes to make the decisions.

Being Jewish, Paul would have understood peace as *shalom*, the wholeness that comes from God. It does not come to condemn but to teach us how to live this new life in Jesus. The false teachers gave their pronouncement, "*Dis*qualified." But the peace of God speaks over us and declares, "Qualified!" God has called us together in one body—the body of Jesus the Messiah—so that we may know and enjoy this peace. This should lead us to a life of continual praise to God, and in a moment, Paul will tell us how we come into that.

Since we are the body of King Jesus, we should be attentive to His word. It is the word that comes from Him that guides us, not the word of angels, or the teachers of the "mysteries," or the superstitions of folk religionists, or lists of rules and regulations. The word of the Messiah is the message of the gospel, the teaching about who He is and why He came, the things He said and did—all that comes from Him and pertains to Him. It comes to fill us abundantly with His wisdom.

With this word and the wisdom it brings, we are to teach and exhort each other. The way we do this, Paul tells us—and here is something we were not expecting—is with psalms and hymns and spiritual songs. This is worship, an activity of the Holy Spirit in us. It is only by the Spirit that we can say, with any conviction, that Jesus is Lord (1 Corinthians 12:3). In his letter to the believers at Ephesus, Paul speaks of this same activity coming as a result of being filled with the Holy Spirit.

> *And do not be drunk with wine, in which is dissipation; but be filled with the Spirit, speaking to one another in psalms and hymns and spiritual songs, singing and making melody in your heart to the Lord, giving thanks always for all things to God the Father in the name of our Lord Jesus Christ. (Ephesians 5:18-20)*

On the night of the Last Supper, Jesus taught that the Holy Spirit would take the things of Jesus and declare them to us (John 16:15). That is, He comes to teach us about Jesus. When we are filled with the Spirit, then, it will always be about Jesus. This is the grace of God at work in our hearts, bringing praise to God. Everything we say and do is to be done in the name of King Jesus the Messiah (not in the name of angels). In this way we give proper thanks to the Father through Him.

Focus Questions

1. How does the peace of God rule in our hearts?

2. In Ephesians 5, it is being filled with the Holy Spirit that leads to psalms, hymns and spiritual songs. Why does Paul emphasize, here in Colossians, that it is being filled with the word of the Messiah that leads to those things?

3. What does it mean to do all things in the name of King Jesus? Why is this important?

New Life in the Home

Wives, submit to your own husbands, as is fitting in the Lord.
Husbands, love your wives and do not be bitter toward them.
Children, obey your parents in all things, for this is well pleasing to the Lord.
Fathers, do not provoke your children, lest they become discouraged.
Bondservants, obey in all things your masters according to the flesh, not with eyeservice, as men-pleasers, but in sincerity of heart, fearing God. And whatever you do, do it heartily, as to the Lord and not to men, knowing that from the Lord you will receive the reward of the inheritance; for you serve the Lord Christ. But he who does wrong will be repaid for what he has

done, and there is no partiality.

Masters, give your bondservants what is just and fair, know-ing that you also have a Master in heaven. (Colossians 3:18-4:1)

When the word of Messiah is at home in us, it fills us with His abundant wisdom. Paul shows us now what this wisdom looks like in our domestic relationships. The form of instruction he uses here is that of the "household code." This form was a common feature of Greek and Roman teaching on ethics. They outline the duties and responsibilities members of a household owed to one another and especially to the *paterfamilias*, that is, the father of the family, the head of the house. In other words, they define how wives should act toward their husbands, children toward their fathers and slaves toward their masters—and it was all rather one-sided.

What Paul does with the household code, however, is unexpected, unheard of, even revolutionary. Household relationships in this new life in Jesus is not a one-way street—it runs *both* ways. We see this not only in this letter but also more extensively in Ephesians 5:21-6:9. Peter has a similar code (1 Peter 2:18-3:9).

Wives are to submit to their husbands. This is "fitting," or appro-priate for our new life in Jesus. Indeed, submitting to one another is appropriate for all of us. To the believers at Ephesus, Paul prefaces his household instruction with the words: "Submitting to one another" (Ephesians 5:21) That is, every believer is to submit to every other believer. *This is revolutionary!*

What does it mean, in practical terms, to submit? French theo-logian Ceslas Spicq offers this explanation:

It means first of all accepting the exact place God has as-signed, keeping to one's rank in this or that society, accepting a dependent status, especially toward God (Jas 4:7), like children who are submissive to a father's discipline (Heb 12:9), after the fashion of the child Jesus. This religious subjection is made up of an obedient spirit, humaneness of heart, respect and willingness to serve. To submit is to accept directives that are given, to honor conditions that are imposed, to please one's superior (Titus 2:9) or honor him by the homage that is obedience (cf. Eph 6:1), to repudiate egotism and aloofness. It is to spontaneously position oneself as a servant towards one's neighbor in the hierarchy of love. (*"Hypotasso," Theological Lexicon of the New Testament.*, Vol. 3 pp. 425-6).

This is the way of the Lord Jesus, "to spontaneously position oneself as a servant towards one's neighbor in the hierarchy of love." And this is the way He instructs us to live, too:

You know that those who are considered rulers over the Gentiles lord it over them, and their great ones exercise authority over them. Yet it shall not be so among you; but whoever desires to become great among you shall be your servant. And whoever of you desires to be first shall be slave of all. For even the Son of Man did not come to be served, but to serve, and to give His life a ransom for many. (Mark 10:42-45)

This is not about becoming a servant so that we may one day be promoted to greatness. No, becoming a servant *is* the promotion. Serving one another *is* greatness. It is the way of love, and the way of God, who *is* love. I call it the *algebra of love*: God is love. Love gives and serves.

For *husbands*, it means that they are now to love their wives and not be bitter or ill-tempered toward them or provoke them. This love is not just a matter of having kind affections toward them. No, this is the kind of self-giving love Jesus has for *us*. Indeed, in Ephesians, Paul adds, "Just as Christ also loved the Church and gave Himself for her" (Ephesians 5:25). Jesus submitted His whole life for the sake of the Church, and that is how husbands are to love their wives, submitting themselves for the sake of their wives. Note also what Paul does *not* say. He does not say, "Husbands, rule over your wives," or "Husbands, make your wives submit."

Children are to obey their parents in all things. This pleases the Lord and is in keeping with the Fifth Commandment: "Honor your father and your mother, that your days may be long upon the land which the Lord your God is giving you" (Exodus 20:12).

But now there also is a word to *fathers*: "Do not provoke your children." Do not be quarrelsome or contentious. Do not push them to anger, for example, by continual fault-finding or dealing unfairly or unreasonably with them. This is so that they do not become discouraged and no longer willing to try, or they dishonor their parents instead of coming to maturity and walking in the favor and blessing of the Lord. The love of King Jesus expressed through fathers has much influence over this.

Now Paul speaks to the relationship between *bondservants* and *masters*. In his letter to the believers in Galatia, he said, "There is neither Jew nor Greek, there is neither slave nor free, there is neither male nor female; for you are all one in Christ Jesus" (Galatians 3:28). In other words, there is full equality for every believer in Jesus, regardless of ethnicity, social stature, or whether one is a man or woman. For *servants and slaves*, this was a new reality, one that undermines abusive institutions. Though they were still servants according to their present social structure, the old system that operated according to the principalities and powers, it was now King Jesus they were really serving. Just as Jesus came to be a servant and offer His life on the cross, and in so doing disarmed the powers, in the same way, those who belong to Him overturn corrupt institutions and power structures by serving as He did.

How much more true this was for *masters* who took Jesus as their own Master. They were now answerable to Him for how they treated their servants. Realizing that Jesus came as a servant Himself for their sake presents a tension that must eventually pull down the walls of corrupt systems. This would be heightened for believing masters who had believing servants—how could they now continue in a system in which they made slaves of their own brothers and sisters? Treating them justly and equitably must ultimately turn out to mean giving them their freedom.

Focus Questions

1. How does the new version of the "household code" Paul presents demonstrate the "disarming of the powers"?

2. How does it demonstrate the new reality of who every believer now is in Jesus?

3. In what ways does it actually change societal structures?

Onesimus and Philemon ~ Receiving a Brother

In the previous section on household relationships, Paul gives extra attention to how slaves and masters who are believers are to share their new life in Jesus. Though he speaks in general terms, he also has some specific individuals in mind. There is a man named Philemon, a faithful follower of King Jesus, who hosts meetings of the church in his home in or near Colosse. At the same time Paul writes to the believers there, he also prepares a brief, personal letter to Philemon. Paul's desire for him is "that the sharing of your faith may become effective by the acknowledgment of every good thing which is in you in Christ Jesus" (Philemon 6).

Philemon has a servant named Onesimus, who ended up in Rome, where Paul is presently imprisoned for preaching the gospel of King Jesus. Most likely, Onesimus had some sort of falling out with Philemon and ran away to make an appeal to Paul, because Paul exercised spiritual oversight for the church at Colosse. This journey took an unexpected turn for Onesimus, however, when Paul led him to faith in Jesus the Messiah.

Paul now writes Philemon seeking a kindly disposition towards Onesimus. He does not speak by spiritual command but by the appeal to love (vv. 8-9): "I appeal to you for my son Onesimus, whom I have begotten while in my chains, who once was unprofitable to you, but now is profitable to you and to me" (vv. 10-11). Paul speaks of him as a son begotten in the faith by Paul himself. In his letter to the believers at Colosse, Paul speaks of Onesimus as a "faithful and beloved brother, who is one of you" (Colossians 4:9).

In Paul's thinking, and indeed in the new reality of King Jesus, Onesimus and Philemon were on equal footing. It was the existing culture and economy—leftovers from the principalities and powers that Jesus disarmed—that needed to be addressed here. The old way of masters and slaves makes no sense to the new life we have in Jesus and so must give way. "I am sending him back," Paul says and then adds, "You therefore receive him, that is, my own heart" (v. 12).

Paul wants Philemon to receive Onesimus, not as a runaway slave who has been returned and is subject to severe treatment, but as dearly and affectionately as Paul himself has received him. An even greater desire, however, is that Onesimus be able to come again to Paul and assist him in the ministry of the gospel (v. 13). But Paul will not do that without Philemon's consent, nor will he compel Philemon to do so (v. 14). His appeal is purely that of love and the way of new life in King Jesus, so that Philemon might receive Onesimus fully as a brother in the Lord.

For perhaps he departed for a while for this purpose, that you might receive him forever, no longer as a slave but more than a slave—a beloved brother, especially to me but how much more to you, both in the flesh and in the Lord. (vv. 15-16)

Though we do not know for certain the outcome of this appeal, it is hard to imagine that Philemon would refuse Paul's request—when you realize that someone is your brother, how can you any longer treat him as anything less? The historical tradition of the Church is that Onesimus was martyred for his faith shortly after Paul's death. He has been canonized as a saint by several Christian communions and is especially remembered every February 15.

Focus Questions

1. Paul wants Philemon to be effective in sharing his faith. How does his request of Philemon play into this?

2. Though Paul had spiritual oversight of Philemon, he did not want to "command" him in this. Why not?

3. What are other ways believers might treat other believers as less than brothers or sisters?

The Spiral of Watchful, Thankful Prayer

*Continue earnestly in prayer, being vigilant in it with thanks-
giving; meanwhile praying also for us, that God would open to
us a door for the word, to speak the mystery of Christ, for which
I am also in chains, that I may make it manifest, as I ought to
speak. (Colossians 4:2-4)*

Paul now moves on from teaching about household relationships
to offer a few words that will help the believers at Colosse keep
properly focused on Jesus.

To "continue earnestly" in prayer means to be devoted to prayer,
attentive to prayer, always ready to pray. The Greek word comes from a
root that means to be steadfast. It is in the present tense and indicates
that our devotion to prayer is to be a continual activity. Elsewhere,
Paul tells us to "pray without ceasing" (1 Thessalonians 5:17).

Prayer is not simply about making requests. It is an act of worship,
pressing into God with all our desires and concerns. It is an activity of
the Holy Spirit at work in us. "For we do not know what we should
pray for as we ought, but the Spirit Himself makes intercession for us
with groanings which cannot be uttered" (Romans 8:26).

Prayer is not just for set times but for the thousand moments of
each day. It is a constant fellowship with God, a running conversation
with Him as we encounter the world together. Nor is prayer a private
activity. We pray when we are together and we pray when we are apart,
but our prayers always belong to each other because *we* belong to each
other, and it is the same Spirit praying in us all.

"Being vigilant" speaks of watchfulness, wakefulness, always being
alert. With all the miracles he performed, Jesus said that He could do
only what He saw the Father doing (John 5:19). He judged only as

He heard the Father judge (John 5:30) and spoke only as the Father showed Him to speak (John 8:28), so that He did only those things which pleased the Father (John 8:29). In other words, He learned how to watch the Father and listen for His voice. The focus of our watchfulness, then, is on the Father, and on Jesus, who shows us the Father. The Holy Spirit is given to help us in this, of whom Jesus said, " All things that the Father has are Mine. Therefore I said that He [the Holy Spirit] will take of mine and declare it to you." Being alert in our prayer to the works of the Father, the things of Jesus and the activity of the Holy Spirit, we will come to the understanding and discernment we need.

As we continue in prayer and watchfulness, we discover how much we have to be thankful for, about King Jesus, how God is working through Him in the world, who He is in us and who we are in Him. Giving thanks to God for all He does and reveals to us brings the cycle of prayer to completeness, spinning our spiral of worship forward. It is in this prayerfulness, this watchfulness, this thankfulness—this worship—that we keep our focus properly oriented on King Jesus.

Paul also wants the believers at Colosse to be sure to remember *him* in their prayers, that God would give him and his associates (whom he will mention shortly) an "open door" for the message of the gospel. His passion is to preach the "mystery" of the Messiah to the whole world, to proclaim that Jesus is not just King of the Jews but the Lord of heaven and earth who has come to bring the *shalom*, the wholeness that comes from God, into all the world. He desires, as he said earlier, "to make known what are the riches of the glory of this mystery among the Gentiles: which is Christ in you, the hope of glory" (Colossians 1:27). It is for this that he has gladly endured the chains of imprisonment, and he has no intention of backing down from it. He wants to make the mystery apparent, that it may be seen by all. And he wants to speak it *boldly* as well as *clearly* (see Ephesians 6:20).

The "open door" Paul seeks might be release from prison so that he can have greater mobility to go forth. But his passion for the good news about King Jesus is such that he is ready for the message to go forth even if he himself remains in chains.

Focus Questions

1. Is devotion to prayer a dull or difficult thing to do, or a source of wonder and amazement for you?

2. How does watching or listening for the Lord play into prayer?

3. Why is thanksgiving important to this kind of watchfulness and prayer?

Walking in Wisdom, Seasoned With Salt

Walk in wisdom toward those who are outside, redeeming the time. Let your speech always be with grace, seasoned with salt, that you may know how you ought to answer each one. (Colossians 4:5-6)

Paul concludes his instructions with a word on how believers should relate to those who do not know King Jesus or understand the faith. "Walk in wisdom toward those who are outside." It is a walk, a consistent pattern, a life of wisdom. Not the wisdom offered by the false teachers, the wisdom that is according to the principalities and powers and how the world has learned to operate under them, but spiritual wisdom—the wisdom that comes from God by the Holy Spirit at work in our spirits.

Ever since Paul heard of their faith, he has prayed for these believers to be filled with wisdom and understanding (Colossians 1:9). This is the wisdom that is able to bring every believer into maturity in our new life in King Jesus (Colossians 1:28). It is the wisdom that is found in Him, "in whom are hidden all the treasures of wisdom and knowledge" (Colossians 2:3). It is the wisdom that abounds to us as we let the word that is from and about Him come and make its home in us.

We are to "redeem the time." The word for "redeem" literally means to buy up from the marketplace. The word for "time" here is not *chronos* but *kairos*. It is not clock or calendar time but poignant time, a time that is ripe, an opportune time. This is not about time management but about preparedness. To redeem the time is to make the most of every opportunity. *Thayer's Greek Definitions* offers this meaning: "to make wise and sacred use of every opportunity for doing good." We do this by walking in the wisdom that comes from God. He will show us what to do or say, just as He showed Jesus.

Our speech, our words, our communication, should always be gracious, "seasoned with salt." Jesus said, "Salt is good, but if the salt loses its flavor, how will you season it? Have salt in yourselves, and have peace with one another" (Mark 9:50). If our words have no wisdom or grace, they will be tasteless and will not go down well, and they might even be spit back at us. When they are seasoned with wisdom, understanding and a gracious disposition, they convey the love of God in a way that might persuade the hearers and lead to their peace. In his letter to Timothy, Paul said, "a servant of the Lord must not quarrel but be gentle to all, able to teach, patient, in humility correcting those who are in opposition, if God perhaps will grant them repentance, so that they may know the truth, and that they may come to their senses" (2 Timothy 2:24-26).

Walking in wisdom and speaking with grace, we will know how to effectively answer those with whom we engage. Peter put it this way, "Sanctify the Lord God in your hearts, and always be ready to give a defense to everyone who asks you a reason for the hope that is in you, with meekness and fear" (1 Peter 3:15). This is about making a *defense*, not about being *defensive*. It is giving an answer, a reason for the expectation we have in King Jesus. This readiness is not especially about studying rhetoric and engaging in debates, although those may be good things to study. It arises from knowing King Jesus the Messiah, who He is and why He came, understanding from the Scriptures what God is doing in the world and walking in the wisdom that comes from God.

Focus Questions

1. What does "wisdom toward those who are outside" look like?

2. Paul speaks of "redeeming the time," or making the most of every opportunity. What sort of opportunities do you think he might have had in mind?

3. What are some examples of speech that is "seasoned with salt"? What are some examples of speech that is not?

Not a One Man Show

Tychicus, a beloved brother, faithful minister, and fellow servant in the Lord, will tell you all the news about me. I am sending him to you for this very purpose, that he may know your circumstances and comfort your hearts, with Onesimus, a faithful and beloved brother, who is one of you. They will make known to you all things which are happening here. (Colossians 4:7-9)

Paul was no one man show. He always had partners with him, a team of associates who worked alongside him in ministry. During the times he was in prison for preaching the gospel, he relied on them all the more. Now, as he brings his letter to a close, he offers a few words about them.

Tychicus is from the province of Asia, in Asia Minor, likely from the city of Ephesus. Luke includes him in Acts 20:4 as one of those who accompanied Paul on his third missionary journey. Paul mentions him in his letter to the Jesus believers at Ephesus, using similar words as here. He is a "beloved brother, faithful minister, and fellow servant in the Lord." Is there a higher acclamation than that? In the Parable of the Talents, the commendation of the Master was, "Well done, good and faithful servant … Enter into the joy of your Lord" (Matthew 25:21, 23). Paul is sending Tychicus to see how they are doing and to let them know what is happening with him.

Onesimus is the slave who ran away from Philemon and wound up with Paul at Rome, where he unexpectedly became a follower of King Jesus. Paul calls him a "faithful and beloved brother" and would like to keep him there with him in Rome because he has become so helpful to the ministry there (Philemon 11-13), but he knows he must send him back home to Colosse to sort out his affairs with Philemon.

Aristarchus my fellow prisoner greets you, with Mark the cousin of Barnabas (about whom you received instructions: if he comes to you, welcome him), and Jesus who is called Justus. These are my only fellow workers for the kingdom of God who are of the circumcision; they have proved to be a comfort to me. (Colossians 4:10-11)

Aristarchus, a Jew of Thessalonica, is another one Luke mentions as part of Paul's missionary team (Acts 19:29; Acts 20:4). He has been faithful through thick and thin. He accompanied Paul on his voyage to Rome, where it appears he was likewise imprisoned. He is known to the Jesus believers at Colosse and they are known to him. The early Greek Church identifies him as one of the "Seventy Apostles" and the bishop of Apamea. Tradition says that he was martyred along with Paul under Nero's persecution.

Mark is John Mark, Barnabas' cousin, or perhaps his nephew (the exact intent of the Greek is uncertain here). He went out with Paul and Barnabas on a missionary journey (Acts 12:25) but soon turned back for home and for some reason did not continue on with them "to the work" (Acts 15:38). Because of that, when Barnabas wanted to bring Mark on another mission, Paul refused. The disagreement between Paul and Barnabas was so sharp over this that they split up, Barnabas taking Mark and Paul taking Silas (Acts 15:37-40). Paul eventually realized that Mark was beneficial to the ministry after all (2 Timothy 4:11). Mark also became very important to the ministry of Peter, who spoke of him as of a son. Early Church history indicates that the Gospel According to Mark represents the preaching of Peter. Paul instructs the church at Colosse, "If he comes to you, welcome him." Perhaps they have been aware of the previous dispute over Mark, and Paul wants them to know that has all now been cleared up. According to Church history, Mark was martyred in the region of modern-day Libya, not very many years after Paul and Peter gave their ultimate witness by blood.

We know very little about "Jesus who is called Justus." Aristarchus, Mark and Justus, the only members on Paul's team who are Jewish, have stood firm with him in difficult times and have proven to be a great comfort for him.

Focus Questions

1. Paul always had people around him who were associated with him in ministry. Why is this important and what are the advantages?

2. How did Paul view their place in ministry—as *under* him, *with* him, both? How did *they* see their place in ministry?

3. Who are you partnered with in the ministry of King Jesus? When things get tough, who are you there to stand with and who is there to stand with you?

Standing Firm

Epaphras, who is one of you, a bondservant of Christ, greets you, always laboring fervently for you in prayers, that you may stand perfect and complete in all the will of God. For I bear him witness that he has a great zeal for you, and those who are in Laodicea, and those in Hierapolis. Luke the beloved physician and Demas greet you. (Colossians 4:12-14)

We met Epaphras at the beginning of this letter, where Paul called him "our dear fellow servant, who is a faithful minister of Christ on your behalf" (Colossians 1:7). Here, we find Epaphras "laboring fervently" for them. This is from the same Greek word Paul uses of himself in Colossians 1:29, about "striving" according to the energizing power of God at work in him. The word is *agonizomai*. Although we get our English word "agony" from it, Paul is not speaking of intense pain but intense effort.

Epaphras has great fire, great passion for the Jesus believers at Colosse. He was the one who first brought them the proclamation about King Jesus the Messiah. He is not now present with them but with Paul in Rome, many miles away. What is his fervent labor for them, then? Prayer. He pours himself out for them in intercession, pressing his desires and requests for them before God. His purpose is the same as Paul's: That they may "stand perfect and complete in all the will of God." Or as Paul put it earlier, to "present every man perfect in Christ Jesus" (Colossians 1:28).

Paul's prayer in Colossians 1:9 is that they would be "filled with the knowledge of [God's] will in all wisdom and spiritual understanding." Epaphras prays that they may *stand* in that, to be firm and confident, to come to maturity and fulfill the divine destiny God has for them. His intense desire is not only for the believers at Colosse but also for those at Laodicea and Hierapolis. He holds all three cities in his heart with great zeal and gladly gives himself for them.

Luke was a Gentile who came to King Jesus, apparently through the ministry of Paul at Troas. He is the author of the Gospel According to Luke, and its companion piece, The Acts of the Apostles. It is not until Acts 16:10-11 that Luke begins speaking of himself as part of Paul's missions (not by name, but by use of "us" and "we"). From then on, he was a fixture of Paul's ministry and was with him near the end of Paul's life. "Only Luke is with me," Paul says in his farewell letter (2 Timothy 4:11).

All we know of Demas are Paul's brief mentions in Colossians and Philemon, which are merely words of greeting, and this bit in 2 Timothy 4:10 that is quite telling: "Demas has forsaken me, having loved this present world." Apparently the growing persecution near the end of Paul's life turned out to be more than Demas was willing to bear.

Focus Questions

1.   Epaphras "labored fervently" in prayer for the believers at Colosse. What do you imagine that was like? How did that intense desire come about in his life?

2.   Who is there for whom you have great zeal and what is your desire for them?

3.   What do you suppose might account for the difference between Epaphras and Demas, or Luke and Demas?

Fulfilling the Ministry of Jesus

Greet the brethren who are in Laodicea, and Nymphas and the church that is in his house.

Now when this epistle is read among you, see that it is read also in the church of the Laodiceans, and that you likewise read the epistle from Laodicea. And say to Archippus, "Take heed to the ministry which you have received in the Lord, that you may fulfill it."

This salutation by my own hand—Paul. Remember my chains. Grace be with you. Amen. (Colossians 4:15-18)

Having passed along the greetings of his ministry associates, Paul now adds a few of his own.

There are close associations between the believers at Colosse and those at Laodicea. For one thing, they are only about ten miles apart. For another, Epaphras actively ministered to both groups (as well as at

Hierapolis). So, although Paul writes to the believers at Colosse, it is natural that he has them extend his greetings to those at Laodicea. Indeed, he wants to be sure that this letter itself will be shared with them all.

"Nymphas" appears to be one of those believers at Laodicea. Though the name in the *NKJV* and some other versions is masculine in form, there are also a number of other versions that render it as feminine, "Nympha," including the *NASB*, *NIV*, *ESV* and *LEB*. The reason for this is that the early copies of this letter speak of the church that meets in "her" house. Because of cultural tendencies, it is more likely that early copyists would have been tempted to change "her" to "his" rather than "his" to "her," so "her" is more likely the original reading.

Churches did not meet in public spaces but in private homes. Nympha's was one. Philemon's was another. Paul's letter to him is addressed, "To Philemon our beloved friend and fellow laborer, to the beloved Apphia, Archippus our fellow soldier, and to the church in your house" (Philemon 1-2). Apphia might have been Philemon's wife, and Archippus their son. The church met in their home.

Paul speaks of a letter he wrote to Laodicea, which he wants to be read at Colosse also, but this has never been conclusively identified. Some have suggested that it is the book of Ephesians, which is very similar to Colossians. Others suggest that it was the letter to Philemon, since he might have been closer to Laodicea and there was a church that met in his house. Or perhaps the letter simply no longer exists.

There is a personal word to Archippus, "Take heed to the ministry which you have received in the Lord, that you may fulfill it." This should not be taken as a suggestion that Archippus has somehow been slack in his duties. We do not know exactly what this ministry entails. Perhaps he is a pastor of the church that meets in his house, or maybe he is filling the position at Colosse left vacant by the absence of Epaphras, and Paul is giving him a friendly word of encouragement in this new role. Church tradition has Archippus as the first bishop of Laodicea and numbers him among the "Seventy Apostles."

Finally, Paul closes his letter with a few words in his own hand. His letters were usually written down by an amanuensis, a secretary of sorts. His own handwritten words were usually brief. Here, they are quite simple: "Remember my chains. Grace be with you. Amen." Paul wants to remind them that he needs their prayers. It is similar to the way the letter to the Hebrews closes, "Remember the prisoners as if chained with them—those who are mistreated—since you yourselves are in the body also" (Hebrews 13:3). The message is that we are all in this together. Paul would also want them to remember that he was in chains for their sake, as well as for the sake of the gospel.

Paul also usually closes with a benediction, such as, "Grace be with you." Simple but profound. It is not merely a custom, though. Paul really has the grace of God in mind, and it is for every believer just as much as it is for him. "Amen" affirms the truth of that grace, and of all he has written to them.

Focus Questions

1. The early Church met in homes. Was this merely because of the times or were there advantages to it?

2. Why did Paul want the church at Laodicea to read the letter he wrote to the church at Colosse? Why is this letter important for us today?

3. What ministry have you received from the Lord and how will you know when you have fulfilled it?

Also by Jeff Doles

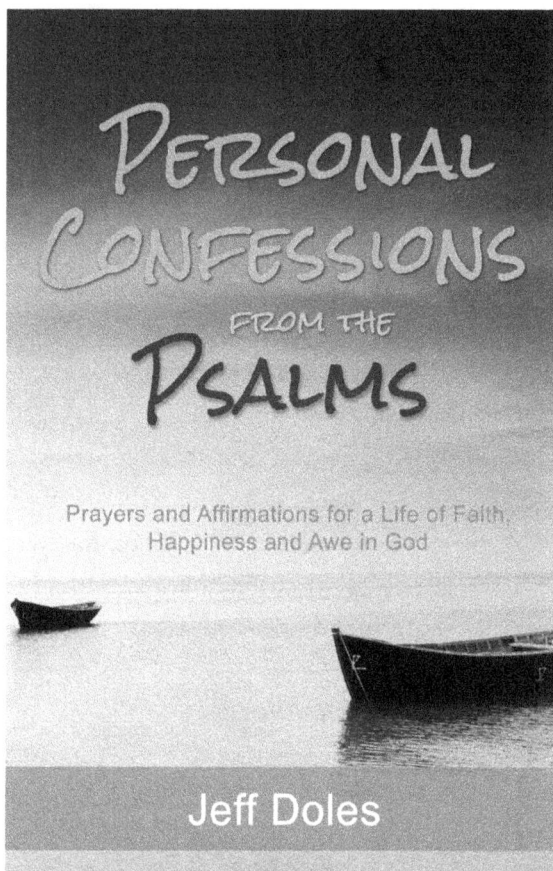

Personal Confessions
from the Psalms
Prayers and Affirmations for a Life of Faith, Happiness and Awe in God

ISBN 978-0-9823536-1-5
5.5 x 8.5 in., 98 pages

Available at www.walkingbarefoot.com

Also by Jeff Doles

Keeping
the Faith
When Things Get Tough

Peter's
Letter
to
Jesus
Believers
Scattered
Everywhere

Bite-Sized
Studies Through
the Book of
First Peter

Jeff Doles

Keeping the Faith
Peter's Letter to Jesus Believers
Scattered Everywhere
Bite-Sized Studies Through
the Book of First Peter

ISBN 978-0-9823536-2-2
5.5 x 8.5 in., 94 pages

Available at www.walkingbarefoot.com

Also by Jeff Doles

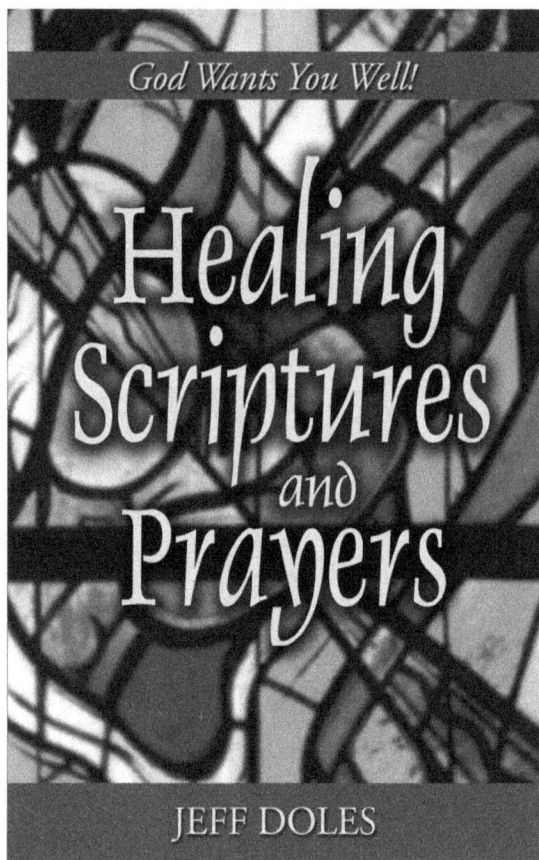

Healing Scriptures and Prayers

ISBN 978-0-9744748-1-6 (Paperback)

6 x 9 in. 120 pages

Available at www.walkingbarefoot.com

Soak in the Healing Scriptures

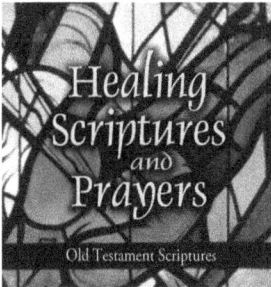

Vol. 1: Old Testament Scriptures

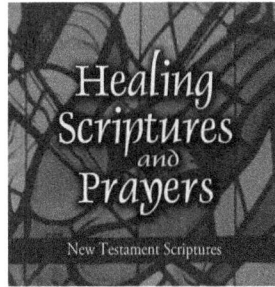

Vol. 2: New Testament Scriptures

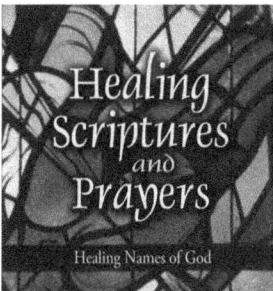

Vol. 3: Healing Names of God

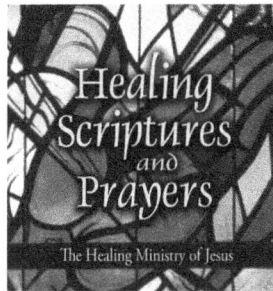

Vol. 4: The Healing Ministry of Jesus

Healing Scriptures and Prayers

Available in CD and MP3
Listen to audio clips and order at
www.walkingbarefoot.com

Also by Jeff Doles

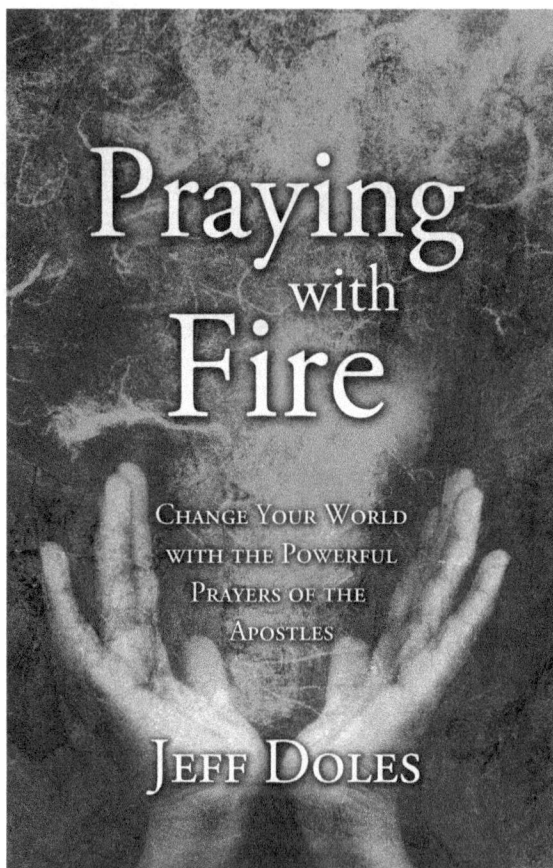

Praying With Fire
Change Your World with the
Powerful Prayers of the Apostles

ISBN 978-0-9744748-6-1
6 x 9 in., 104 pages

Available at www.walkingbarefoot.com

Also by Jeff Doles

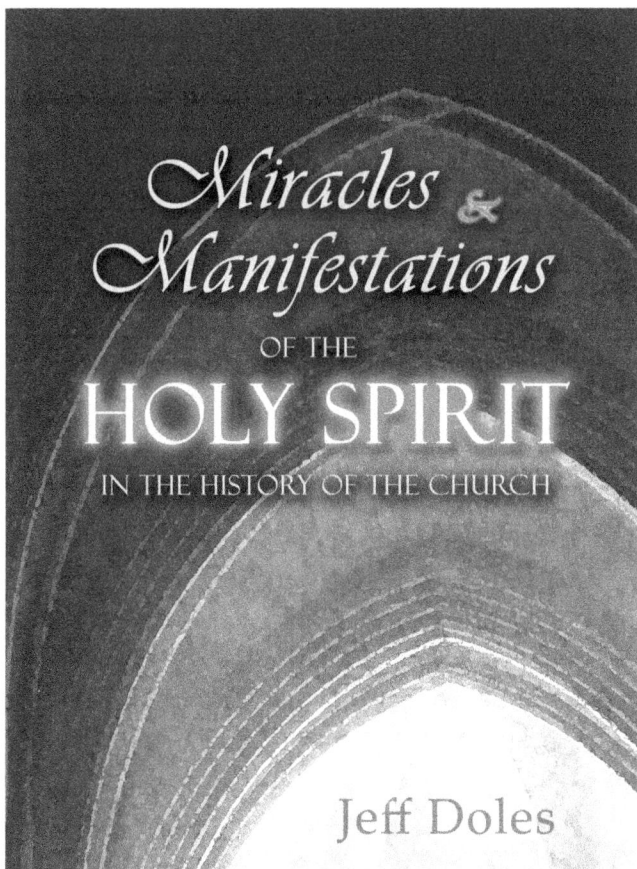

Miracles and Manifestations of the Holy Spirit in the History of the Church

ISBN 978-0-09744748-9-2
9.6 x 7.4 in., 274 pages

Available at www.walkingbarefoot.com

Also by Jeff Doles

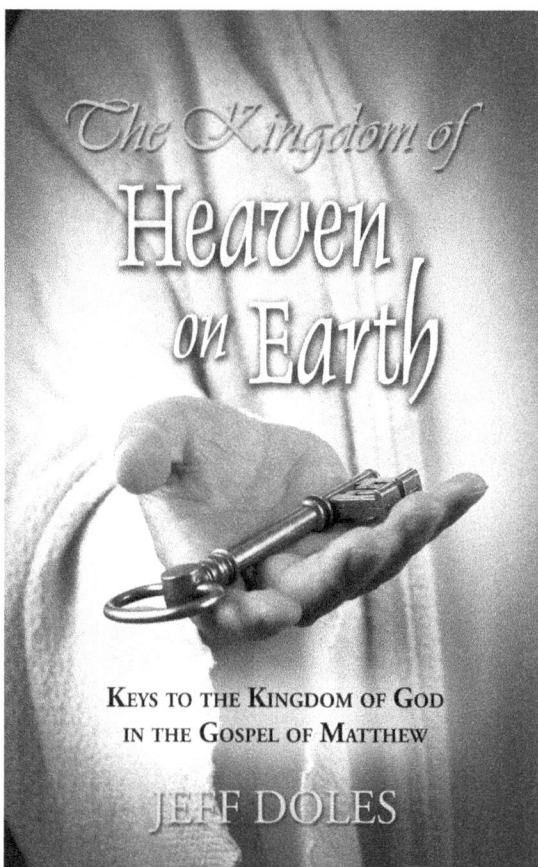

The Kingdom of Heaven on Earth
Keys to the Kingdom of God
in the Gospel of Matthew
Bite-Sized Studies in the Book of Matthew

ISBN 978-0-9823536-0-8
6 x 9 in., 194 pages

Available at www.walkingbarefoot.com

Also by Jeff Doles

God's Word in *Your* Mouth
Changing Your World Through Faith

ISBN 978-0-9744748-8-5
6 x 9 in., 140 pages

Available at www.walkingbarefoot.com

Also by Jeff Doles

On This Pilgrim's Way
A Walking Barefoot Hymnal

Available in CD and MP3
Listen to audio clips and order at
www.walkingbarefoot.com

Also by Jeff Doles

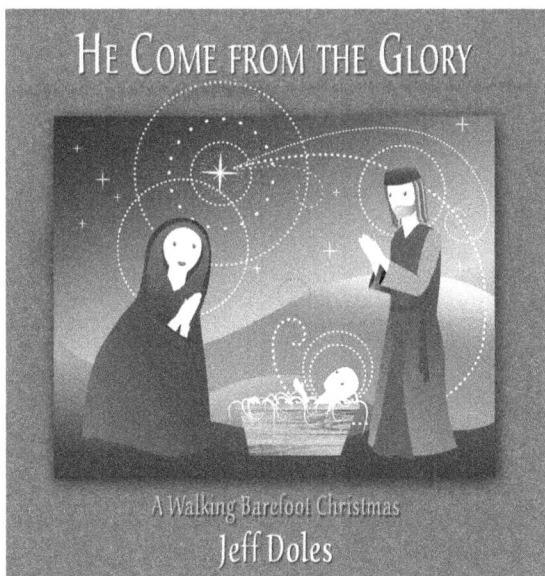

He Come from the Glory
A Walking Barefoot Christmas

Available in CD and MP3
Listen to audio clips and order at
www.walkingbarefoot.com

www.ingramcontent.com/pod-product-compliance
Lightning Source LLC
Chambersburg PA
CBHW031623040426
42452CB00007B/641